COLLECTOR'S CHOICE

BECOME THE INTELLIGENT INVE$TOR

15 EASY-TO-FOLLOW LESSONS PLUS SELF-TESTS

BONUS 5 STARTER PORTFOLIOS ARE INCLUDED

JOHN F.CICOTTE

LifePhase Publishing

Published in the United States of America by LifePhase Publishing

First Edition

10 9 8 7 6 5 4 3 2 1

Library of Congress Control Number: 2025917032

ISBN: 978-0-9993484-2-0 (Paperback)

ISBN: 978-0-9993484-3-7 (eBook)

Interior Design by Booknook.biz.

Disclaimer and Notice

The purpose of this course is to educate and inform. The author has drawn from a wide range of reputable sources to ensure the information is as accurate and current as possible. However, laws, regulations, tax codes, investment practices, and retirement strategies can and do change. Readers are encouraged to stay informed and consult qualified professionals before making legal, tax, insurance, financial, or investment decisions.

This course provides readers with a foundational understanding of investment planning. It is offered with the understanding that neither the author nor the publisher is providing legal, tax, insurance, financial, or investment advice. The author and publisher expressly disclaim any liability for loss or risk, direct or indirect, that may arise from the use or application of the information contained in this course.

This is not a "get-rich-quick" guide or a manual for day trading. If you do not fully understand the investment process do not put your money at risk.

If you are a financial professional questioning traditional methods that no longer feel right, *Become The Intelligent Investor* offers a fresh perspective. Drawing on over 30 years of real-world experience, it delivers practical insights and strategies to help you manage risk—and spark those "aha" moments that come from seeing the bigger picture.

An Important Introduction

Congratulations on your foresight and ability to take proactive steps to secure your financial health now and in retirement! ***Become The Intelligent Investor*** is an investment course you'll keep on your desk and refer to often over the years as you navigate the complicated world of investing.

Become The Intelligent Investor will guide you through fifteen easy-to-follow lessons and self-tests, along with five suggested starter portfolios, to help you make educated and sensible decisions about how to invest your money.

Some of the topics you will study:

- Should you be a do-it-yourself investor or hire a pro?
- How to overcome your first investing problem—COMPLEXITY, it is the enemy of execution
- Learn from history—2008 Case Study
- How to measure risk
- How to control risk
- How to invest with mental clarity
- Determining where you stand money-wise
- The M word to cure stress and anxiety is not merchandise; it's money

- The Warren Buffett money directive
- Understanding investment fees, disclosed and undisclosed
- And much more

Hello, My Name Is John

Cicotte (sea-cot). My career in the financial services profession began in 1973. I answered a blind newspaper ad for a job that offered a draw against commission. It was a major life insurance company in Phoenix, Arizona. To my extreme disappointment, I failed their aptitude test. Determined, I returned to explain why they were making a mistake. My explanation made sense to them, so they hired me.

They were pleased with my performance, so I was promoted to sales manager after six years. A company move to California in 1983 caused me to re-examine a large firm's corporate and political structure, and I realized it wasn't client-centric to my satisfaction. Due to their flawed client paradigm, I decided to establish an independent financial and retirement planning practice.

In 1987, I qualified as a Certified Financial Planner™ (CFP®). I was determined to become the kind of professional who could truly help people plan for retirement. I quickly realized that tax implications were tied to just about every investment decision, and if I wanted to give solid advice, I needed to understand them. So I studied tax law for two years (not exactly a fun subject). In 1989, I became an Enrolled Agent (EA), a designation issued by the U.S. Department of the Treasury.

My business plan was always to die with my boots on. I loved working for my clients. However, in 2017, my doctors gave me a life-changing diagnosis and said moving to a dry, warm climate could minimize a debilitating health condition. With deep reluctance, I decided to sell my practice in 2018, retire as a CFP® and EA, and move back to Arizona. It was the right decision, and the change has allowed me to continue enjoying financial and retirement planning by sharing my knowledge with you.

Contents

Acknowledgments

A special thank you to my wife, Carol, for her continued validation and encouragement. She was supportive when I converted our kitchen table into my writing desk. She gracefully offered ideas to incorporate into this course, making your journey toward a positive outcome possible.

There's an extraordinary group that has contributed immensely to this study course—my former clients. Though too numerous to name, they have each played a vital role. Their unwavering confidence, trust, and loyalty inspired me to learn as much as possible so I could meet their expectations, offer sound advice, and protect their investments. To each of you, I am deeply grateful.

During the latter half of my career, I often thought that I needed to distill everything I had learned, evaluated, accepted, rejected, and refined into a simplified investment course, so that others could benefit from the knowledge I had gained and receive the best possible counsel.

When I finally started writing, I needed critical feedback. Beta-readers are worth their weight in gold. But when writers call on friends to serve in this capacity to evaluate their manuscripts, they face one main problem: these folks don't want to hurt the writer's feelings. In my case, these brave souls openly and honestly offered critical feedback, vastly improving what you hold in your hands. I am grateful to Jim Farr, Gregory Brown, Anita Solano, Monica Elertson, Brent Adams, Daryl Scheans, and Jody Leber-Pay. Students of this course will experience a better outcome because of your contributions. To say 'thank you' is inadequate, so please know that I genuinely appreciate your help in bringing this fifteen-year mission to fruition.

All authors must engage with a professional editor. To do anything less would be a disservice to readers. As you study these lessons, you will experience a smooth simplicity that makes learning almost automatic. It is thanks to the skilled editing of Tracy Hart (www.editingwithhart), who is a real pro. Tracy's skill reversed my writing flaws and made this course more manageable for the reader.

The often-overlooked aspect of any refined hardcover, paperback, or eBook is the precise interior formatting that ensures every element flows seamlessly. Fortunately, A.I. led me to Judith at www.booknook.biz. Talk about professionalism—she and her team embody the kind of excellence that built America's greatest companies. Their strong work ethic gave me the confidence to present you with this distinctive learning system.

After completing this course, you may be surprised to learn that I hired a professional investment advisor upon retirement. Tom Chandler, *CFP®, RICP®, CIMA®, CPWA®* is my advisor. He shoulders the technical direction of my portfolio, offers common-sense suggestions on portfolio alignment, and allows me to focus on enjoying my life in retirement.

Tom is a Certified Financial Planner professional (CFP®) and Retirement Income Certified Professional (RICP®). He has also earned the CPWA® and CIMA® credentials from the Investments & Wealth Institute™ in conjunction with the University of Chicago Booth School of Business and the University of Pennsylvania Wharton School.

When referring to how he became a financial professional, he said, *"My passion is clear. My career in finance and investments began in 1993 when I witnessed a close family member have financial difficulties later in life. Since then, I have made it my mission to help others avoid the same outcome.*"

His review of this course and careful attention to perfecting each of the book's lessons added to my confidence in your learning experience. Thanks a million, Tom.

What you are going to learn

Investing in the stock market is a gamble. Investors who fail to measure their risk concentration properly may experience a financial disaster.

Lessons One—Five will help all investors build a solid financial foundation.

Lessons Six—Fifteen will help you nail down a comprehensive strategy for how and where to invest your money, while also teaching you how to measure and control investment risk in the process.

In Lesson 14, you'll learn what I believe is your *number one problem* as an investor. It's a predicament that Wall Street rarely discusses or teaches. It may be the most relevant component of your entire investment style—and it applies to most investors, regardless of age.

This isn't a study course you'll read for personal pleasure and entertainment. Instead, ***Become The Intelligent Investor*** is a no-nonsense investment course. There's no fluff. It's power-packed, concise, and to the point. Every word was carefully chosen to make your learning experience simple, fun, revealing, and rewarding. **Your first read will take about two and a half hours.** After reviewing some lessons, self-tests, and your notes, you can build a portfolio based on your concerns about measuring and controlling investment risk. You can begin with one of the starter portfolios provided in Lesson Twelve.

Each lesson contains need-to-know and need-to-remember information that you should identify, internalize, and apply. I recommend you start your learning experience this way. Keep your laptop, some sticky notes, a highlighter, and a pen and paper handy. Then, write comments on everything you want to remember. Highlight concepts, rules, and procedures you want to implement and track for your portfolio.

The self-test following each lesson reinforces your learning and **guides you through the practical implementation process using fill-in-the-blank and true-or-false questions.** It's designed to get you up and running with what may become your ideal investment portfolio. **While this course does not imply or guarantee a successful outcome, it will help you understand how to allocate your money effectively and how to measure and control investment risk.**

Study these lessons to become familiar with and control your investment ecosystem as a do-it-yourself investor. However, you may be like many investors who don't want to tackle the investment process but want to understand what your financial advisor is doing with your money. **This course will provide you with the knowledge to collaborate with and ensure that your advisor's recommended plan is tailored to your needs.**

Author's Special Message: Four Pivotal Building Blocks

Though many of the basic principles of smart investing are available online, and credibly so, the guidance offered in this course will give you a thorough, comprehensive understanding not available elsewhere. You must have a solid foundation before you build anything of consequence, whether a house or an investment portfolio. The four **"must-read"** building blocks below will prepare you for a smooth, in-depth learning experience as you complete each of your lessons.

1. Learn from History—Case Study 2008

Throughout my career, I have accumulated a wealth of knowledge to help you learn from history. Sharing them has been my goal for many years.

Whether you're investing for a short-, intermediate-, or long-term goal—or for retirement—this case study will give you clear insight into my thought process as I managed money for my clients. You're about to discover what three decades of experience have taught me as you build your investment portfolio—a system I believe will be perfect for you.

For example, many of my clients were retired, and a key concern I had for them was their "time horizon." (Your time horizon is the time before you need a pre-determined lump sum or when you want to start taking distributions, and the number of years you'll need to continue cash flow.) Neither my clients nor I could predict how long they would live. Longevity is a significant consideration. They could live for thirty years or more after retiring. Their paychecks stopped when they retired. Some didn't have other sources of income to offset investment losses. Their stockpile of money had to last the rest of their lives. My job was to protect—and hopefully grow—their nest eggs. Caution was my guiding principle.

This concern for other investors, like you, motivated me to formulate these 15 Lessons. I want to help you save, accumulate, and protect your investments by creating a common-sense investment strategy that you can understand and manage with minimal effort.

To help you understand what I've learned through trial and error during a long career, you must know how I think. **The following case study will put you inside my brain.**

I need to take you back to the fall of 2007 to explain the technique I employed to help protect my clients' investments—and their emotions. The following portfolio strategy will be as effective now as it was then.

The Financial Crisis, also known as the Great Recession, began in October 2007, as the S&P 500 (short for Standard & Poor's 500, a stock market index that tracks the daily performance of the 500 largest publicly traded U.S. companies) was on the verge of losing 55% of its value. In January 2007, a barrel of oil cost $53.52 (data from IndexMundi.com). By early 2008, some commodities experts were predicting that oil could rise to $200 a barrel. If they were right, the stock market would suffer big losses, and so would clients' accounts. Instead of coaching everyone to sit tight, the industry mantra, I recommended moving into corporate bonds to sidestep the stock market's possible slide.

The price of oil continued to rise until it peaked at $138.83 in

July of 2008. Then it started dropping fast until it reached $41.34 that December. I had moved my clients into corporate bonds in early August. The experts had been wrong, and we dodged a bullet. My clients' accounts weren't affected, and they felt secure because they knew I was watching over their money.

More bad news soon rattled the stock market. On September 15, 2008, Lehman Brothers filed for bankruptcy. The next day, the Federal Reserve took control of American International Group (AIG), the world's largest insurance company. It was mind-blowing; Lehman Brothers was a 128-year-old company, and AIG had billions in assets. What was happening?

If you remember these events, do you remember how you felt? I do. **I was scared for my clients' nest eggs.** I didn't know what was happening or its cause, but somehow, I knew it would worsen. I had a gut feeling. Even though I had just repositioned client portfolios, my staff and I got on the phones. The message to clients: "John is afraid the stock market will sustain significant damage, and he recommends moving out of stocks and, this time, into U.S. Treasuries." Since my clients had complete confidence in me, they gave permission.

As a result, **those clients missed the 22% plunge in the S&P 500** in the first two weeks of October, and their U.S. Treasuries had a positive return in the fourth quarter. The S&P 500's 55% slide lasted until March 2009. I repositioned client portfolios in the first week of May once I thought the conditions were favorable.

With 20/20 hindsight, you must agree that moving out of stocks in the middle of September was a piece of good fortune. Many clients said I was their hero. One told me, "Mary and I listened to our country club friends commiserating about how much money they were losing, and we just sat quietly with smiles."

Colleagues said, "John, you're a rock star." One admitted, "I wish I had the guts to do what you did, John."

I wasn't a hero or a rock star. My mission was to set in motion a strategic thought process to help protect clients' wealth, which you'll learn about in detail before you finish this course.

2. Learn How to Measure Investment Risk

Here's a question of great consequence: Does your portfolio expose you to too much or **not enough risk?** The most critical underpinning of a sensible investment plan is learning how to measure your willingness to accept risk, or what I want you to think of as your "sleep-number"—the percentage of your investment funds that you are comfortable losing before you begin to lose sleep over it and take drastic actions to sell, possibly prematurely. **In Lesson Six,** you'll perform a crucial exercise to determine what risk level you feel is acceptable. That result will be your sleep-number. This formula will make it easier to decide whether to hang in there when the stock market goes south, to reposition assets, or go to the sidelines.

Whether new to investing, a veteran investor, or somewhere in between, this course will teach you how to measure investment risk. It will also transform your approach to investing, enabling you to do so with greater confidence, reduced worry, stress, and anxiety.

3. Learn How to Control Investment Risk

Learning how to measure investment risk is paramount, but it is also essential to learn how to control it.

You're about to discover a straightforward tactic that will give you confidence whether the stock market is soaring or crashing. You'll also acquire a solid understanding of the essential elements the everyday investor must understand and employ. The most important of which is controlling investment risk.

4. Learn How to Invest with Mental Clarity

This course will teach you how to invest with mental clarity. It's an innovative, simplified investment logic for the everyday investor. You're not going to study Puts, Calls, and Covered Straddles. Why? Because you're an *investor*, not a *trader.* There is a critical distinction between the two. *Investors* invest long-term, but due to their emotions, they sometimes think short-term, which is a significant mistake. *Traders* need to think in the short term, sometimes on a daily basis. Please imprint these differences in your memory bank. Mull over this concept often as you journey through this new learning experience—and particularly when you're watching the financial report on TV. Why? Because, as an *investor*, you're in it for the long haul. The convoluted financial news speaks to *traders*, those poised to react instantly. For *investors*, following such advice could lead to inappropriate changes in your portfolio.

You must be proactive and employ good information to make sensible investment decisions. You intend to protect your money, so you demand better ideas. You want information you can process without getting a degree in higher economics. You're perceptive, and you've decided to *Become The Intelligent Investor*. You want to learn a down-to-earth approach that teaches you how to *invest with mental clarity.* Read on, and in about two hours, you'll be studying real investment eye-openers. Each one will boost your confidence and help you attain the ability to *invest with mental clarity*.

It's time to get started. Keep reading, take notes, and highlight everything you want to remember. You can *Become The Intelligent Investor.*

LESSON ONE

Do-It-Yourself or Get Help?

ARE *YOU* GOING to tackle your investment pursuits, or do you want someone with whom you can discuss ideas and strategies? Remember this: you don't know what you don't know. Don't fool yourself into thinking you do. If you want help, you have lots of choices. You can evaluate stockbrokers, insurance agents, Certified Financial Planners™, financial advisors, others with alphabet soup after their names, Robo Advisors, or your brother-in-law who says he's an expert (don't believe him unless he has studied this course, internalized, and implemented its teachings).

Whether you pursue this critical challenge to manage your investments and retirement nest-egg with this course as your companion or hook up with a financial advisor, your choice should be well thought out. Regardless, you can always change your mind.

Here are some factors to consider as you decide whether to take the wealth-building journey on your own or work with a professional:

1. Do you feel comfortable with numbers, and do you enjoy organizing the information you gather?
2. Realistically, do you have the time to commit to consistently staying focused on this crucial task?
3. Are you the type of person who maintains focus over time, or do you get bored with things once you've learned them?
4. Do you feel excited at the prospect of learning enough to make your own decisions about your financial future?
5. Would it feel less anxiety-provoking if the decision wasn't only your own? Meaning, would you welcome sharing the responsibility with a trusted professional?

If you choose the latter, your search for a trusted investment professional can begin by asking relatives, friends, and coworkers about their experiences. It isn't an easy task, but it's where you should start. Remember: you have a choice in whom you hire. So, before you decide, check out the ones you're considering.

Here are websites to help you:

- CFP.net/search/
- plannersearch.org/
- brokercheck.finra.org/ and sec.gov/
- NAPFA.org/
- Wiseradvisor.com/

As you study each lesson, you'll strengthen your resolve to *Become The Intelligent Investor.* Return to this lesson often to inventory your needs, wants, wishes, and obstacles. You're not juggling daggers, but you are juggling all elements of your financial life. You need to consider your short-, intermediate-, and long-term goals.

✓ Record your thoughts and ideas from this lesson that you want to incorporate into your investment strategy.

Self-Test Lesson One

Do-It-Yourself or Get Help?

Whether you pursue this critical challenge as a do-it-yourself investor or hook up with a financial advisor, your choice should be well thought out.

(Are you studying this course on an e-reader? No problem—just use a notebook to keep track of your answers.)

1. How would you score your level of investment expertise on a scale from 1 (novice) to 10 (expert) TODAY? ________
    a. Come back and answer this question after studying and implementing this course ________
2. Will you manage your investment pursuits yourself, or would you prefer to work with someone who can discuss ideas and planning strategies with you?
    a. I'll tackle them myself. ________
    b. I'll hire a professional. ________

3. If you checked (b) above, do the following:
   a. Talk to relatives and friends who have advisors about their experiences and whether they have had positive results. Write their names down here.
      Advisor #1 ______________________________
      Advisor #2 ______________________________
      Advisor #3 ______________________________

Search for the advisor's background online. Check off each when completed:

- www.CFP.net/search/
- www.plannersearch.org/
- www.napfa.org/
- www.sec.gov/
- www.wiseradvisor.com

Inventory your:

Needs: ______________________________

____

____

____

____

Wants: ______________________________

____

____

____

____

Wishes:

Obstacles

LESSON TWO

Target an Unbendable Savings Goal

IN MY THIRTY years as a Certified Financial Planner™, I found that many people put off investing a portion of their earnings to help make their financial dreams come true. Have you put your savings for the future on the back burner? Why?

Albert Einstein, considered by many to be one of the most intelligent humans ever to live, said, **"Compound interest is the eighth wonder of the world. He who understands it, earns it . . . he who doesn't . . . pays it."** Translation: save your money.

Cultivating the habit of paying yourself before you pay others will give you a sense of financial muscle, dominance, and control. Have you mastered this discipline? If your answer is no, **Lesson Five** will teach you how to adjust your thinking to make this invaluable practice possible.

Choosing the path of least resistance and doing nothing leads to failure. ***So, don't let the thorny uncertainties ahead stop you from reaching for your rose.*** Visualize your dreams and manage your money to make them a reality. And regardless of your age, you have a dream. Do you think about it often? Can you describe it in detail? If you answered, "I don't know," take some time right now and give it serious thought. Most dreams are rooted in money, even when they are noble in nature. Is your vision materialistic, educational, for professional gain, or to help others? Your answer doesn't matter. You must have money to make it happen.

Plotting your financial future takes deep thought. Are you a take-charge, younger person who knows it's never too soon to ignite your spark, or are you retired or close to retirement and asking yourself, "What will the rest of my life look like?" Tap into your innermost feelings and beliefs to find your answer.

Close your eyes and visualize your life after work. What do you see? What do you want to do? Uncover your dream. It may be hiding in the back of your mind. What would you like to achieve? Please write it down in positive terms and attach it to your bathroom mirror. Read it every day.

"How do I overcome common obstacles and capture my dream?" you ask. Conquer your first planning problem—complexity. It's the enemy of execution. **Complexity fuels procrastination** and crushes your good intentions. Fortunately, this course will simplify the complex challenge of investing, enabling you to overcome procrastination.

✓ Record your thoughts and ideas from this lesson that you want to incorporate into your investment strategy.

Self-Test Lesson Two

Target an Unbendable Savings Goal

Cultivating the habit of paying yourself before you pay others will give you a sense of financial muscle, dominance, and control. Have you mastered this discipline?

1. Do you save money from every paycheck?
   a. Yes ______
   b. No ______
2. Can you "see" the long-term value of saving money?
   a. Yes ______
   b. No ______
3. Do you have a short-, intermediate-, or long-term goal(s)?
   a. Yes ______
   b. No ______

Here are some examples. Put your thinking cap on and come up with what is meaningful to you. Shade the circles that apply.

Short-Term Goals (1-3 years)

- Initiate a Savings Plan—Deposit three months' income.
- Build an Emergency Fund—Save six months' worth of expenses.
- Create and Stick to a Budget—Track income and expenses to avoid overspending.
- Pay Off High-Interest Debt—Focus on credit cards and personal loans first.
- Improve Credit Score—Pay bills on time and reduce credit card expenses.

Intermediate-Term Goals (3-10 years)

- Save for a Major Purchase—Like a car, vacation, or home down payment.
- Invest for the Future—Open an account and start investing in Mutual Funds, Exchange Traded Funds (ETFs), or actively managed index funds.
- Contribute to Retirement Accounts—Start an IRA or contribute to a qualified retirement plan early to take advantage of compounding growth.
- Eliminate Student Loans—Develop a plan to pay them off faster.
- Increase Financial Literacy—You're doing that by studying this course, but don't stop there; cultivate a learning habit.

Long-Term Goals (10+ years)

- Realize Financial Independence—Work towards having enough savings and investments to have muscle, dominance, and control over your future.
- Buy a Home (if desired)—Save for a down payment and maintain a good credit score.
- Plan for Family and Kids—Save for future expenses, such as education.
- Start a Business—If entrepreneurial, set aside funds and develop a plan.
- Build Wealth—Invest in assets that grow over time, like real estate and stocks.

Describe your goals if you checked yes to number 3 above.

Short-term objective(s):

Intermediate-term objective(s):

Long-term objective(s):

What is your "time horizon" (i.e., the time before you need a pre-determined lump sum or when you want or need to start taking distributions and the number of years you'll need to continue cash flow) for each objective?

Short-term objective: Date to achieve ____
Intermediate-term objective: Date to achieve ____
Long-term objective: Date to achieve ____

LESSON THREE

Know Where You Stand Money-wise

TAKE INVENTORY. GET a paper and a pen or use your laptop and write down how much money you have in savings, an emergency fund, and investments. You must know where you stand money-wise.

Your answers may look bleak if you're 25. Don't despair. If you're 75, you might be surprised at how much wealth you've accumulated. Regardless of your age, knowing your financial situation is essential. A solid financial foundation looks like this:

1. Savings should equal a minimum of three months of your monthly gross income;
2. an Emergency Fund requires an amount equal to six months of gross income; and

3. your investments should equal how much muscle, dominance, and control you want over your life. The more money you have, the more power.

There is no magic in the above three categories. They're benchmarks you can use to target what makes the most sense to you. Focus on an amount that gives you a feeling of safety, confidence, and security. If your car breaks down, it's not an emergency. So, get the repair cost from your savings. If you lose your job, tap into your emergency fund, which gives you six months of breathing room. The key to financial happiness is "saving" money, not spending it. **If you need help**, Lesson Five will teach you how to make this life-changing savings maneuver.

I know what you think if you're 75. This doesn't pertain to me. Okay, then talk to your children and grandchildren about how they can build a solid, worry-free financial life. **Tell them the "M" word to cure their stress and anxiety isn't merchandise—it's money.** You're right; it's not an easy conversation. But give it your best effort. It's another way to let them know you love them.

✓ Record your thoughts and ideas from this lesson that you want to incorporate into your investment strategy.

Self-Test Lesson Three

Know Where You Stand Money-Wise

A solid financial foundation looks like this:

1. Savings should equal a minimum of ______ months of your monthly gross income.
2. An Emergency Fund requires an amount equal to ______ months of gross income. You may think these building blocks will be challenging to put in place, but you can do it!
3. Your savings/investments should equal how much muscle, dominance, and ______ you want over your life. The more money you have, the more power and control you will enjoy.
4. Complete the following:
    a. Three months of income equals $ ______
    b. How much money do you have in savings? $ ______
    c. Do you have a deficit or surplus? ± ______
    d. Six months of income equals $ ______

e. How much money do you have in an emergency fund? $ ______
f. Do you have a deficit or surplus? ± ______
g. How much money do you have in your muscle, dominance, and control fund? $ ______
h. Do you have a deficit or surplus? ± ______

5. The "M" word to cure stress and anxiety isn't ______ - it's ______.

LESSON FOUR

Lay a Rock-Solid Financial Foundation

LIFE IS COMPLEX; many components are central to a life of pleasure and happiness. The one I encourage you to focus on is establishing or reinforcing a rock-solid financial foundation.

So, how do you protect your financial life? When you are still employed and think about it with a clear mind, your most prized and productive asset is your ability to work and earn a living. You insure your car and your home. You should also ensure a continuous income for yourself and those who depend on you, with disability and life insurance. This is the financial base you should build first. Think about it as the horse in front of the cart. Protecting your investments is also necessary, which is why I created this course. When you have these building blocks in place, you can focus on accumulating money and having fun.

Wisdom to embrace: soon after I was born, my father's doctor told him he wouldn't survive five years if he didn't change his dietary lifestyle. He didn't listen to his doctor's advice, and five years later, he died at age 39. My father didn't believe in insurance. A co-worker took up a collection to raise enough money so my mother could pay for his funeral. He had no savings, which created additional complications. As a result, the authorities took me from my mother and put me in a foster home. My childhood would have been much better if my father had put responsibility before pleasure. He married at the age of 24 and took on the obligation of providing for a family, but didn't fulfill his duty. I've never forgiven him and never will.

Today, a healthy 24-year-old non-tobacco user can invest in a $500,000 low-cost, bare-bones "term life" insurance policy for approximately $30 per month. It's pure insurance protection. Talk to a life insurance agent to get information and calculate the amount of money that those you love and who depend on you financially would need to be protected in case of your untimely passing. Hard to think about, sure, but as my own life attests, vital to provide.

When you discuss your life insurance needs with an insurance agent, don't let the agent convince you to buy "whole life insurance." The pitch is convincing. After a "number of years," the policy builds savings, also known as cash value, that you can borrow against or withdraw. The whole life policy is only appropriate after you have established your savings account, emergency fund, disability insurance, and investment portfolio.

Be aware, there is a situation described by the term 'living death'. It's when you become disabled. You can't work and are no longer productive, but you must still eat and pay bills. You remain a consumer, but you are no longer a provider. Disability insurance pays for your fixed expenses, maintains your financial health, and buys you self-respect.

Prioritize an adequate amount of disability insurance as part of your fixed expenses. It's one of the critical building blocks in your rock-solid financial foundation.

Do you live in one of the five states or territory below that provide State Disability Insurance (SDI)? If you do, don't count on it, as qualifying for SDI can be difficult, and you may not be eligible. The specific disorders to qualify for SDI benefits vary by state, and the benefit period for these states is limited to 26 to 52 weeks, depending on the state.

- California
- Hawaii
- New Jersey
- New York
- Rhode Island
- Puerto Rico

And please don't count on the Social Security Administration's disability insurance program. It has a complicated definition of disability. You must not be able to perform the work of any occupation.

Be aware of this principle: You must purchase insurance before needing it. If you wait too long, you may not qualify. When people wait until they need insurance, it's called adverse selection against the insurance company. The concept of everyone putting money into the pot to provide required benefits fails because there are too many sick and dying participants. You must be in good health when you request benefits. So, don't wait. Make this critical investment part of your fixed outflow.

✓ Record your thoughts and ideas from this lesson that you want to incorporate into your investment strategy.

Self-Test Lesson Four

Lay a Rock-Solid Financial Foundation

Here's an important question: How do you protect your financial life? When you think about it with a clear mind, and you're still employed, your most prized and productive asset is not your money—it's your ability to work for a living and earn money.

1. Do you have homeowners/renters' insurance?
   a. Yes ___________
   b. No ___________
   If you answered no, date to complete: ___________
2. Do you have auto insurance?
   a. Yes ___________
   b. No ___________
   If you answered no, date to complete: ___________
3. Do you have disability insurance?
   a. Yes ___________ No ___________
   b. If you answered no, date to complete: ___________

4. Do you have life insurance?
   a. Yes __________ No __________
   If you answered no, date to complete: __________

Did you answer no to any of the above? If you did, convert them to yeses ASAP. Keep this in mind: you must purchase insurance before you need it. You can't wait for a broken leg, fire, or a car accident to invest in insurance. Disability and life insurance are the same; you must invest in them before an event occurs. If you wait too long, you might not qualify.

LESSON FIVE

Follow This Buffett Directive

WARREN BUFFETT SAID, "Don't save what is left after spending; instead, spend what is left after saving." Good advice, huh? Here's the snag. How can you, your children, and your grandchildren create the footing necessary to acquire financial peace of mind and a safe economic zone when, like many Americans, the paycheck runs out way before the month's expenses?

The key to transitioning to a happier and financially secure lifestyle is to become adaptable. **Your mind is powerful,** and you can adjust your habits to align with a new, positive thought pattern. You've heard it before: you must **pay yourself before paying anyone else.**

You might say, "Hey, John, how can I save when my outflow exceeds my income?"

Think about this: what would you do if you went to work next

Monday and your boss said, "I have bad news. I must let you go. You're a valuable employee, but the company is in a predicament. I've no choice; the economy is shrinking the company's cash flow, and I need to reduce expenses by 15%. If you can adjust to a reduction in pay, your job is safe."

What would you do? Start looking for a new job or make the necessary financial adjustments?

If you said you would adjust, then you *can* save 15% of your income and pay yourself before paying anyone else. Save first, cover all fixed expenses and then spend what is left.

Look at the big picture. Have you ever thought about how much you will earn before you retire? **Do this: multiply your current annual income by two, then multiply the result by the number of years until you expect to retire.** It'll be a lot of money. How much do you plan on having left to fund your retirement? How will you live if you spend all your money before you retire? Don't plan on Social Security because it'll just supplement your fixed expenses. And don't say you'll start saving next year, because next year never comes.

Instead of becoming broke when you retire, achieve financial independence by reducing your current spending by 15% (20% is even better). Send those dollars ahead to a time when they can help support your vision of a happy, fun-filled retirement. Dollars are like rabbits—put them together and they grow. You should position your money to work for you, rather than letting it work for someone else. If this idea resonates with you, don't put off taking positive action. **Start saving now**. Begin with a low amount if necessary. Then, work your way up. Make a pre-planned commitment to increase your savings to 20%. Set deadlines to fulfill your promise of achieving financial freedom.

Remember what Einstein said: "Compound interest is the eighth wonder of the world." You earn interest on your savings/investments, and then you earn interest on the interest. Investing $5,000 per year in a tax-qualified (before-tax) account at a 7% annual return rate for 30 years results in a total of $472,304. If you wait 10 years to start, the total is $204,977. See what I'm talking about? This total grows exponentially when you add more money each year.

Here's a way to determine how to adjust your spending to achieve your goal. On paper or in a computer document, create two columns. Title the left column, Essential (fixed) Expenses and the right, Discretionary (pleasure) Expenses. Next, get your checkbook and credit card statements and begin listing each expenditure as either Essential or Discretionary. To fine-tune this process, keep track of all cash purchases for a 30-day period. Add them to the appropriate column in your ledger.

When all of your expenses have been compiled, examine your list of Discretionary (pleasure) Expenses. What can you reduce or cut to come up with a meaningful percentage to move to savings? Perhaps you should ensure that you pay your credit card bill within 30 days. **Following this rule saves you from paying exorbitant interest rates.**

In my 30 years of experience working for clients, one of their most significant challenges was taking inventory of their cash outflows. What about you? **I promise it will be an enlightening exercise.** When you finish listing your expenditures, you'll be able to develop your financial power and control by moving non-essential outflows to your savings and investments. Easy peasy. You're right; easier said than done. But you can do it. Start now. Soon, you'll get a handle on how satisfying it is to invest and accumulate money. Controlling your spending habits gives you the power to achieve your dreams.

✓ Record your thoughts and ideas from this lesson that you want to incorporate into your investment strategy.

Self-Test Lesson Five

Follow This Buffett Directive

Your eventual goal is to save 20% of your annual gross income.

1. What percentage are you saving from each paycheck? _____%
2. What is your target percentage? _____%
3. What is the difference between the two? _____%
   a. Increase your savings percentage in pre-planned stages if necessary. Today _____%
   b. In 6 months _____%
   c. In 12 months _____%
4. Here's an interesting thought. How much money do you think you'll earn during your working lifetime? Multiply your current income by 2. Then multiply the result by the number of years until your planned retirement. Your total is the best guess projection of how much money you will earn. Of course, this is a ballpark estimate to give you an idea of the enormity of your

earning potential. Perhaps you have never thought about this before. It's a big number!

Current annual income	$ ____________
Multiply by 2	X ____________
Projected average annual income	$ ____________
Number of years until retirement	X ____________

Projected earnings during your working life. $____________

How much of the total do you want to be waiting for you when you start your forever vacation? $____________

LESSON SIX

Calculate Your Sleep-Number

BEFORE CALCULATING YOUR sleep-number I want you to learn about mistakes that are avoidable that you should be on the lookout for each time you make an investment decision. **Important rule**, keep it simple, and don't go too far into the weeds. Remember what I said earlier—this course isn't going to teach you about puts, calls, covered straddles, or other complex financial instruments. **Your goal is to master a basic system to accumulate wealth.** Otherwise, you might make avoidable mistakes. Here's a list of some of the most common:

- Ignoring Diversification—Investing all your money in a single stock, sector, or asset class increases risk.
- Not Having a Plan—Investing without clear goals and a strategy can lead to poor decisions.

- Trying to Time the Market—Even professionals struggle with this; consistent investing usually wins out in the long term.
- Paying High Fees—Expense ratios, trading fees, and commissions can eat into profits.
- Letting Emotions Drive Decisions—Fear and greed can lead to panic selling or reckless investing.
- Not Rebalancing Your Portfolio—Over time, assets drift from their original allocation, increasing risk.
- Neglecting Taxes—Failing to consider tax implications can reduce returns, especially in short-term trading.
- Investing in what you don't understand—Buying stocks, crypto, or funds without knowing how they work is risky.
- Not Thinking Long-Term—Frequent trading and short-term thinking often lead to losses.

All of the above are critically important. However, the one I want you to focus on now is how to diversify your portfolio. Before you learn how to protect your money from a stock market crash, you must learn how to divide your cash into various investment funds or asset categories (see Lesson Twelve). Investing isn't rocket science unless you want it to be. However, instead of rocket science, this course teaches you a down-to-earth investment system. The process is like an easy 50-piece puzzle, not a configuration of 5,000 pieces of confusion.

To make informed decisions about allocating your investment dollars, you must tackle a complex assessment. You need to determine your sleep-number. **In other words, what is your risk tolerance level?** How much loss can you stomach before you, as the industry refers to it, capitulate? When your fear of loss becomes unbearable. You can't sleep, so you sell all of your stocks, cut your losses, and go to the sidelines.

This sleep-number question is hard to answer, but you must do it. Getting this wrong is another avoidable mistake. And a BIG one. **Getting it right may allow you to weather market storms and sleep better at night.**

The industry has a glut of psychological questionnaires to help investors gauge their emotional responses to losing money. There are two critical defects with these questionnaires. The first glitch is that they're hypothetical, and the second is that the investor often completes the questions in a non-emotional state. In other words, the answers will likely be significantly different when the stock market is going south.

Forget about the speculative surveys. Try my method. As an example, use $100,000. Write this number down on a sheet of paper. Assume the stock market is turning red, and you've lost 10%. Write down $10,000 and subtract it from the $100,000. Your balance is $90,000. How do you feel? Will you stay the course, or is your "worry-meter" hitting the red zone and creating fear of higher losses? Deduct $5,000 more as your value drops 15% to $85,000. Get my point? Keep going. Role-play this process as best you can. Feel the losses in your gut. Watch your balance as it continues to slide. At what loss level do you give in to your "worry-meter" and capitulate?

This exercise helps you identify your risk level or "sleep-number" and gain a better understanding of how you'd react in real-time as the stock market loses your money. You should perform this exercise annually, typically in January. As time passes, your feelings about taking on risk may change, and when and if that happens, adjust your sleep-number category accordingly.

Look to recent history as you complete this exercise. In October 2007, the S&P 500 began its downward spiral, and by March 2009, it had plummeted 55% (a result of the financial crisis). If you applied that number to the above assignment, you would have about $45,000 in your account. Would you have capitulated at some point as the stock market plummeted or waited for the rebound? If you said you would've waited, you're a Determined Investor. On the other hand, you may have surrendered to your emotions and sold all your stock after a 28% loss.

Keep this in mind: there is always a rebound. The question is, how deep will the loss be, and how long will it take to bounce back, enabling you to recoup your money? Oh, and yes, can you control your emotions while waiting? ***Controlling your emotions is the most critical element of your entire investment journey.***

Although the total sleep-number categories could be adjusted to create several more, you can start by focusing on the five listed below.

After calculating your sleep-number, you'll see examples in Lesson Twelve of how to invest your money in diverse asset sectors. Identify your sleep-number every January, and then stick with it. Your sleep-number is a personal decision; you know what's best for you and your money.

Sleep-Number Chart

1 – Careful Investor	Up to a 9% loss is acceptable
2 – Engaged Investor	Up to a 17% loss is acceptable
3 – Traditional Investor	Up to a 26% loss is acceptable
4 – Seasoned Investor	Up to a 36% loss is acceptable
5 – Determined Investor	Any loss is acceptable

The number of years before your retirement is an important consideration. Your answers to the sleep-number questions in this lesson might indicate you're a Seasoned investor. Still, that portfolio might be too aggressive for you if your retirement is approaching in the short- or intermediate-term. Perhaps you should use a more conservative portfolio, such as the Traditional or Engaged investor allocation, which you'll see in Lesson Twelve.

✓ Record your thoughts and ideas from this lesson that you want to incorporate into your investment strategy.

Self-Test Lesson Six

Calculate Your Sleep-Number

It's time to calculate your sleep-number. Complete the following worksheet. Calculate the loss percentage from the worksheet below, and then find your sleep-number classification from the Sleep-Number Chart above.

Fill in the blank lines, reducing the portfolio value by 10% and 5% as indicated. Keep going. When you feel your stomach churning, it'll be time to capitulate. When you finish, you'll have the information you need to understand your feelings about risk.

Portfolio Value	$100,000
Market Decline 10%	
Balance	
Market Decline 5%	
Balance	
Market Decline 10%	

Balance	
Market Decline 5%	
Balance	
Market Decline 10%	
Balance	
Market Decline 5%	
Balance	
Balance	
Market Decline 10%	
Balance	
Market Decline 5%	
Balance	

Start by subtracting your ending balance from $100,000. (**If you already have a portfolio, feel free to use your actual numbers.)** The result shows how much you've lost.

Next, calculate your loss percentage: divide the total loss by the original portfolio amount, then multiply by 100.

Example: $14,500 ÷ $100,000 × 100 = 14.5%. That would place you in the *Engaged Investor* risk category.

Finally, your *sleep-number percentage* will help guide how much you should invest in each asset class.

LESSON SEVEN

Growth and Value Stocks

THE MOST BASIC aspect of investing in stocks is to know that the reason a company sells shares of stock is to create a way to raise funds to maintain its financial health. This may take the form of research and development, including the purchase of innovative equipment or professional talent. When a person becomes a shareholder, they accept a stake in the company and invest their money in the products or services the company offers to the country or the world. The viability, strength, leadership, and most importantly, profit-making record of a company figure into the stock's valuation—how risky or not it would be to give the company your hard-earned money. **To become a savvy investor,** you must learn some fundamental principles before proceeding. We'll start with this lesson's compelling investment concept: growth versus value stocks.

Benjamin Graham was a professor at Columbia University, and during the Crash of 1929, he lost a significant amount of money. His loss and intellectual qualities motivated him to explore how he might invest with a higher margin of safety. His research prompted him to develop what became a popular and well-respected game plan, and as a result, the investment world **crowned him the Father of Value Investing.** One of his most famous students is Warren Buffett, the Oracle of Omaha.

To help you better understand this concept, I want you to learn about the deep-seated differences between 'Growth and Value' investing styles, so study as much as possible through online research. When you do, your confidence as an investor will advance.

Growth stocks are stocks of companies that usually don't pay dividends. Instead, those dollars are used to develop and expand the company's market share. Amazon (AMZN), Tesla (TSLA), and Alphabet (GOOGL) are companies that don't currently pay dividends. Instead, they plow profits into expanding their market share. These enterprises have higher expected earnings and sales growth rates, based on their historical performance. Investors buy these shares expecting the stock price to increase so they can sell at a profit.

On the other hand, **value companies pay dividends**, and experts consider their share prices less volatile than those of growth companies. Johnson & Johnson (JNL), PepsiCo (PEP), and ExxonMobil (XOM) are examples of firms that currently pay dividends. Investors, typically those seeking income, purchase these shares. However, keep this thought in mind: there are exceptions to every rule. Strategies could change.

(Whether investing in Growth or Value, I prefer ETFs over individual stocks. Broad diversification and index investing are the key reasons.)

After extensive research and analysis, Benjamin Graham and his associate, David Dodd, **determined that some stocks—whether Growth or Value—are overvalued, and others are undervalued.** This contradicts what some investors believe in—the "Efficient Market Hypothesis." They argue that any company's stock price is always fair because all the information needed to determine its share value is in the public domain. However, others, like Benjamin Graham, believed this hypothesis was flawed. The flaw results from "emotional investors" buying or selling stocks without considering information in the public domain, which means some stocks sell for more or less than their intrinsic value.

Ask ten financial professionals at a broker-dealer conference for the definition of intrinsic value, and you might get ten different answers. A more straightforward concept I want you to consider is what I call "pure value." **What is the pure value of a stock?** It's the company's total assets minus its liabilities—also known as total indebtedness—which results in the stock's book value. This book value is then divided by the number of outstanding shares to determine the book value per share. Or its pure value. Here's an example: XYZ Company has $79 million in assets, $39 million in liabilities, and 1 million shares outstanding. Do the math, and you'll find that the pure value per share of XYZ stock is $40. When XYZ sells for more than $40 per share, it's considered overvalued; if it sells for less than $40, it's undervalued.

Remember, just because a growth stock is overvalued doesn't mean it's a poor investment. It may have an exceptional ability to increase in value. And just because a stock is undervalued doesn't mean it's a winner. It may be undervalued for a good reason.

Graham and Dodd would've analyzed XYZ's profit potential by utilizing other metrics to determine its viability as a long-term investment. **For example,** if XYZ were selling for less than its pure value, they would have wanted to know what caused investors to sell their shares, forcing the price to drop. Bad news or the expectation of bad news is the reason. Before investing in XYZ, they would analyze other data to determine the validity of the talk on the street, thereby determining whether investors were right or, as is often the case, overreacting.

Graham and Dodd are no longer with us. Instead, a new, modern-day group of professional women and men championing both investing styles has replaced them. And you don't have to worry about those metrics today; instead, invest in a quality mutual fund or ETF with a growth or value style objective and let the experts calculate the metrics for you.

So, which is a better investment? The truth? There is no single answer everyone can agree on. Although logic strongly favors the value style of investing, the last decade has perplexed value investors. Some experts say value investing is suspect.

* * *

Institutional Investor is a leading international business-to-business publisher focused on international finance, and it publishes premium journalism, newsletters, and research. An article in The Institutional Investor by Ms. Julie Segal, dated October 24, 2019, provides helpful insight. She writes: Portfolio managers that invest in undervalued stocks have lagged funds that hold growth stocks over the past decade—leading some market commentators to speculate that value investing is dead.

Not so fast, argues asset manager Dimensional Fund Advisors. Ms. Segal's excellent account continues by providing vital evidence to help answer this concern. In the past 10-year period ending September 2019, Dimensional points out that the US growth style recorded a 14.7 percent annualized return rate. At the same time, the US Value style recorded 11.4% increase. Thus, value underperformed growth by a large margin.

* * *

A notable data point in this article is that the growth style outperformed its annual average by 3.4%, while the value style had a yearly return in line with its average. Value still provided investors with a considerable increase in appreciation during those ten years.

What should you learn from these facts? Is **value** investing dead? No, of course not. Value is usually less volatile, but not always. You're not trying to beat a benchmark. You want to grow your money, offset taxes and inflation, and protect your investments with as little risk as possible.

As you can see, **growth stocks performed exceptionally well from 2010 to 2019**. But if you look back at the previous decade, the story was very different. If you had invested in growth-style stocks on January 1, 2000, and checked your account ten years later, you likely would have been disappointed—your investment would have lost value. That decade reminds us that even strong-performing styles can go through long periods of underperformance.

Now, if you study the period from **2019 through mid 2025**, you'll see just how unpredictable the stock market can be. One standout group, known as the **Magnificent Seven**, drove much of the market's growth during this time. These companies include:

- Apple (AAPL)
- Microsoft (MSFT)
- Alphabet (GOOG/GOOGL)

- Amazon (AMZN)
- Meta Platforms (META, formerly Facebook)
- Nvidia (NVDA)
- Tesla (TSLA)

You may be asking yourself: *"How should I invest my money?"*

Should you focus on growth stocks? Value stocks? Or split your investment between the two?

Here's where your personal comfort level comes in.

To get started:

- Refer to how you answered the **Sleep-Number Questions in Lesson Six**. These help you determine your risk tolerance.
- Then, use the **recommended allocation percentages in Lesson Twelve** to divide your investment between growth and value—based on your sleep-number.

This approach gives you a solid starting point, grounded in both your personal comfort and a long-term investment strategy.

You may want to check the current trend. Is growth outperforming value or the opposite? Does the trend favor one or the other? Use your good judgment to determine if you should adjust the percentages in Lesson Twelve.

Always remember that history is not a guarantee of future results.

✓ Record your thoughts and ideas from this lesson that you want to incorporate into your investment strategy.

Self-Test Lesson Seven

Growth and Value Stocks

Investors must understand certain fundamentals of investing. One of the most critical aspects is categorizing stocks as either Growth or Value.

1. Growth stocks are stocks of companies that usually __________ pay dividends.
2. On the other hand, __________ stocks pay dividends, and the experts consider their price per share less volatile than growth companies.
3. After extensive research and analysis, Benjamin Graham and his associate, David Dodd, determined some stocks are __________ and others are __________.
4. Some investors believe in the "Efficient Market Hypothesis." They argue that any company's stock price is always __________ because all information needed to determine its share value is in the public domain.

5. Graham and Dodd believed this hypothesis was flawed. They felt that some stocks sell for less than their ________ value.
6. The definition of intrinsic value is hard to define. A more straightforward concept I want you to consider is what I call "________ ________."
7. How do you calculate the intrinsic value of a stock or its pure value?
    a. Total ________ minus ________ (book value) is divided by the number of outstanding stock shares, which equals a single share price. Or its pure value.
8. When a growth stock is overvalued, it's a poor investment.
    a. True ________ or False ________
9. When a stock is undervalued, it's a winner.
    a. True ________ or False ________
10. Keep this in mind: just because a growth stock is ________ does not mean it's a poor investment, because it may have an exceptional ability to increase in value.
11. And just because a stock is ________ doesn't mean it's a winner because it may be undervalued for a good reason.
12. You don't have to worry about ________; instead, invest in a quality mutual fund or ETF with a growth or value style objective and let the experts calculate the metrics for you.
13. Is value investing ________? ________, of course not.
14. Growth stocks performed exceptionally well from ________ to ________.
15. The previous ________, the story was very different.

16. If you had invested in ________-________ stocks on January 1, 2000, and checked your account ten years later, you likely would have been disappointed—your investment would have ________ value.
17. Now, if you study the period from ________ through mid 2025, you'll see just how ________ the stock market can be.
18. One standout group, known as the ________ ________, drove much of the market's growth during this time.
19. Should you focus on ________ stocks? ________ stocks? Or ________ your investment between the two?
20. Refer to how you answered the ________-________ ________ in Lesson Six. These help you determine your risk tolerance.
21. Then, use the recommended ________ ________ in Lesson Twelve to divide your investment between growth and value—based on your ________-________.
22. This approach gives you a solid ________ point, grounded in both your personal ________ and a long-term investment ________.
23. History is not an indication of future results.
    a. True ________ or False ________

LESSON EIGHT

Learn Fixed-Income Basics

FIXED INCOME (CASH and bonds) is something you must understand, at least on a fundamental level. Bonds are mysterious, especially if you get into the weeds, which we must do right now, but just low weeds.

So, what is a bond? It is a contract between an issuer **(who is the borrower)** and an investor **(who is the lender)**. For example, a bond is issued by a corporation, municipality, or government agency when borrowing money from an investor.

First, let's consider why most investors invest in bonds. The quick answer is that they don't want to risk investing all of their money in stocks and they want annual income. Bonds are generally considered less risky and produce a steady income. Perfect.

A bond's "Term to Maturity"—years until its monetary value is available—ranges from 5 to 30. The shorter the time, the lower the coupon (interest) rate. When bonds are held to maturity, the borrower will pay the investor the bond's face value (loan amount), assuming the organization is solvent.

Bonds come in various sizes and shapes, tailored to the issuer's needs and the company's credit rating. Standard & Poor's Global Ratings, Moody's Investors Service, and Fitch Ratings are three primary bond rating agencies that utilize their rating systems. For example, the **Standard and Poor's "Investment Grade"** scale is—AAA, AA, A, BBB; the "Speculative Grade"—is BB, B, CCC, CC, C, and D.

The **Investment Grade** rating identifies enterprises with a solid financial position and a stable balance sheet. A triple-A rating reflects borrowers with strong balance sheets, while a triple-B rating applies to borrowers in good fiscal shape, but not as financially sound. A company's financial strength—or lack thereof—directly affects how much interest it must offer to attract investors.

Investment Grade bonds pay a lower interest rate than the Speculative Grade, are less risky, and aren't as volatile as stocks. However, risks include possible issuer insolvency, default, inflation, interest rate increases, and the "call option."

"Speculative Grade" or **"Non-Investment Grade"** are designations for companies with weaker balance sheets. The bonds issued by these firms are often referred to as "high yield" or "junk" bonds. **They can be as volatile as stocks,** but they will offer a higher interest rate to attract investors.

Here is an example of how a bond transaction might work. ABC Corporation is expanding and requires $22 billion to fund its project, anticipating that it will become profitable within 15 years. Banks don't have such large sums to lend for an extended period. Instead, ABC Corporation would turn to long-term investors. For various reasons, bond issuers are only willing to make interest payments during the bond's life or term, fifteen years in our example, before repaying the principal (i.e., the loan amount).

Bond investors seek **"fixed income"**—a regular stream of interest payments. It's a match made in heaven: both parties get what they want. The investor receives interest payments they can count on during the fifteen years, assuming the issuer remains in business and doesn't "call" the bond. Interest payments are paid semi-annually. When the bond matures, the issuer, if solvent, will pay the bondholder the outstanding loan amount.

The **"call option"** mentioned above allows the issuer to refinance their loan portfolio when interest rates decline or their credit rating improves. They may call the bond and repay the principal earlier than the original term to maturity. You would implement the same strategy if you had a six percent home mortgage interest rate and then rates dropped to four percent.

Look out for the weeds: When interest rates rise, the value of your bond (price) decreases. Here's why:

When you buy a bond, you're promised a fixed interest payment (coupon). For example, a $1,000 bond with a 4% interest rate yields $40 per year.

Now, imagine new bonds are issued, but interest rates have risen to 6%. These new bonds pay $60 per year.

Why would someone pay full price for your bond that only pays $40, when they could buy a new one that pays $60?

They wouldn't—unless your bond is discounted.

To compete, the price of your 4% bond must fall so its yield matches the new 6% environment. That's how bond prices adjust:

- If your bond's price drops to about $667, then a $40 annual coupon equals a 6% yield—now it's competitive again.
- If you sell your bond before it matures, you may receive less than you originally paid.
- But if you hold to maturity, you'll still get the full face value (unless the issuer defaults).

✓ Record your thoughts and ideas from this lesson that you want to incorporate into your investment strategy.

Self-Test Lesson Eight

Learn Fixed-Income Basics

Fixed income (cash and bonds) is something you must understand, at least on a fundamental level.

1. Fixed income is a combination of __________ and __________.
2. What is the general reason most investors invest in bonds? Because bonds are considered to be less __________, and they produce __________.
3. What is a bond? It is a contract between an issuer/__________ and an investor/__________.
4. Bonds are issued by a __________, __________, or __________ agency.
5. A bond's "__________ to __________" or years to maturity ranges from 5 to 30.
6. Bonds come in different sizes and shapes based on the issuer's __________ and their __________.
7. Name the three primary ratings agencies.

a. ____________________
b. ____________________
c. ____________________

8. What are Standard and Poor's
   a. "Investment Grade" scales?
      i. ________, ________, ________, ________
   b. Speculative Grade?"
      i. ________, ________, ________, ________, ________, ________
9. The triple-A rating depicts borrowers with ________ balance sheets, and the triple-B rating is for borrowers in good fiscal shape but ________ as financially healthy.
10. The financial strength, or lack thereof, dictates how much ________ the borrower would pay to attract investors. "Speculative Grade" or "Non-Investment Grade" are designations for companies with ________ balance sheets. The bonds issued by these firms are commonly referred to as "________ - ________" or "________" bonds.
11. The "________ ________" allows the issuer to refinance their loan portfolio when conditions permit.
12. When interest rates rise, the value of your bond (price) ________.
13. Look Out for the Weeds.
    a. When you buy a bond, you're promised a fixed interest payment (coupon). For example, a $ ________ bond with a ________ % interest rate yields $ ________ per year.
    b. Now, imagine new bonds are issued, but interest rates have risen to ________%. These new bonds pay $60 per year.

c. Why would someone pay ______ ______ for your bond that only pays $ ______, when they could buy a new one that pays $60?

d. They wouldn't—unless your bond is ______.

14. To compete, the price of your 4% bond must ______ so its yield matches the new 6% environment.
15. If your bond's price drops to about $ ______, then a $40 annual coupon equals a 6% yield—now it's competitive again.
16. If you sell your bond before it matures, you may receive ______ than you originally paid.
17. But if you hold to maturity, you'll still get the full ______ ______ (unless the issuer defaults).

LESSON NINE

Mutual Funds or ETFs?

BEFORE YOU DIVE into building your ideal portfolio in Lesson Twelve, the first step is deciding whether to use mutual funds, exchange-traded funds (ETFs), or a mix of both. Sure, you can search online for options with strong track records—but to choose wisely, you need to understand the key differences between them. Each comes with its own advantages and drawbacks, and knowing these will help you select the approach that best fits your goals.

What is a mutual fund, and how does it work? A mutual fund is an investment tool that pools investors' dollars to gain greater leverage when buying stocks, bonds, or money market instruments—and manages those investment choices on behalf of investors. There are two primary business models: 1) a professional manager picks each stock, whether buying or selling, and 2) a group of investment professionals makes the same buying and selling decisions. In either case, thorough analytical research is undertaken. These professionals examine many companies to make a best-efforts assumption about which ones have praiseworthy growth possibilities. **As a result,** mutual funds are "actively" managed. Keyword—**actively**. The fund manager or the team buys and sells stocks trying to "beat the market," like the S&P 500. Mutual funds have higher fees and, in taxable accounts, higher taxes because fund managers attempt to outperform the market by making frequent trades. ETFs model static portfolios, and trades are rare.

The first mutual fund, **Massachusetts Investors Trust,** became available on March 21, 1924. For various reasons, mutual funds have been the primary investment vehicle for most investors. They combine investors' dollars to make investing possible and to satisfy a high investment minimum that may be too costly for an individual. Mutual funds offer a variety of asset categories worldwide, which the industry considers a form of diversification. It's the rule not to 'put all of your eggs in one basket,' and it's a crucial investor command.

What is an Exchange-Traded Fund (ETF)?

Like mutual funds, ETFs offer broad diversification, easy accessibility, and low minimum investments. But there are four key differences:

1. **Lower fees** – ETFs typically cost less to own.
2. **All-day trading** – They trade like individual stocks during market hours, while mutual funds trade only after the market closes.
3. **Passive management** – Most ETFs track a specific index, meaning they hold a set group of stocks and change little over time.

4. **Tax efficiency**—Limited trading within the fund often results in lower taxable distributions in non-retirement accounts.

The very first ETF was launched by State Street Global Advisors on January 23, 1993.

Over time, the stock market has experienced an enormous increase in value, and nothing suggests its unpredictable climb will not continue. Your decision to take advantage of the stock market's irregular rise and fall makes sense if you have an adequate time horizon. **Do you remember what a time horizon is?** It's the future date when you'll need to start spending your money, and the number of years you'll require a cash flow to last through your retirement. The longer you delay accessing your funds, the better your portfolio's opportunity to recover after a down market. Always remember, when your time horizon is short, your investment selection should be more conservative.

You can copy the model of any asset allocation portfolio suggested in Lesson Twelve, using mutual funds, ETFs, or a combination, and include many asset choices depending on your judgment and goals.

When you choose a mutual fund or ETF, **you naturally look at past performance**—even though it doesn't guarantee future results. Still, it's a useful factor to consider. A strong track record is a positive signal, and common sense helps steer you away from consistently poor performers.

The sleep-number exercise in Lesson Six helped you pinpoint how you feel about risk, and the result will assist you in determining your portfolio's percentage of stock and fixed income. **You must make this critical decision before entering Wall Street's casino.**

✓ Record your thoughts and ideas from this lesson that you want to incorporate into your investment strategy.

Self-Test Lesson Nine

Mutual Funds or ETFs

1. Before you put your mind to building your perfect portfolio in Lesson Twelve, you must choose __________ __________ or __________ __________ __________ (ETFs).
2. To make an informed decision, you need to understand the __________ __________ between the two.
3. A mutual fund is an investment tool that __________ investors' dollars to have greater __________ when buying stocks, bonds, or money market offerings – and __________ the investment choices for investors.
4. There are two primary business models:
   1) a __________ __________ picks each stock, whether buying or selling, and
   2) a __________ of investment professionals performs the same buying and selling decisions.
5. Mutual funds are "__________" managed.

6. The fund manager or the team buys and sells stocks, trying to "__________ __________ __________," like the S&P 500.
7. Mutual funds have higher __________ and, in taxable accounts, higher __________ because fund managers are trying to beat the market by making trades. ETFs model __________ portfolios and trades are rare.
8. The first mutual fund, Massachusetts Investors Trust, became available on March 21, 1924. For various reasons, mutual funds have been the primary __________ __________ for most investors.
9. Mutual funds combine investors' dollars to make investing possible without satisfying high __________ __________.
10. Mutual funds offer various asset categories worldwide, which the industry refers to as __________.
11. It's the rule not to 'put all of your __________ __________ __________ __________,' and it's a crucial investor command.
12. The fund manager or the team buys and sells stocks trying to "__________ __________ __________."
13. There are four key differences in Exchange Traded Funds:
    a. **Lower fees** – ETFs typically __________ __________ to own.
    b. **All-day trading** – They trade like __________ __________ during market hours, while mutual funds trade only after the __________ __________.
    c. **Passive management** – Most ETFs track a specific __________, meaning they hold a set group of __________ and change little over time.
    d. **Tax efficiency** – Limited trading within the fund often results in lower __________ distributions in non-retirement accounts.

14. What is a time horizon?

    ____
    ____
    ____
    ____

15. Remember: when your time horizon is ________ your investment selection should be more ________.
16. When you choose a mutual fund or ETF, you focus on past results, which isn't a ________ of future performance.
17. The ________-________ exercise in Lesson Six helped you pinpoint how you feel about risk, and the result will assist you in determining your portfolio's percentage of ________ and ________ ________. You must make this critical decision before entering Wall Street's casino.

LESSON TEN

Control Costs at All Costs!

WHEN YOU INVEST your hard-earned money, you expect it to increase in value; however, you must recognize the risk vs. reward concept. The greater risk may translate into more reward *or* more loss.

Although stock market risk can devastate the value of your account, **there is another way you can experience a surprising loss in value exorbitant fees and other expenses.** Therefore, you must control all costs.

You should never buy a "load" (commission-based) mutual fund. It's an investment that charges a percentage of the invested amount up front. For example, a one-time charge of five percent of your investment is lost before the other 95 percent is invested. Instead, invest in a no-load mutual fund or ETF.

You're wise, and you know nothing of value in life is free—keyword 'value.' As you invest, you'll pay a fee and want value for what you pay.

Stocks, bonds, mutual funds (no-load), and exchange-traded funds (ETFs) are some of your choices. Expect a cost associated with each.

When you hire a fiduciary advisor **(a no-commission advisor),** she will still charge a fee as compensation for her expertise and her broker/dealer who processes trades, administration and oversees the fiduciary responsibility of the advisor. A standard annual management fee for invested assets is 1-2% (sometimes negotiable).

Do-it-yourself investors save on management fees, but they miss out on the expertise of a trained professional. Over time, working with the right advisor could lead to better results.

There are other fees, and when they're less than 1%, they're expressed in basis points or bp (pronounced as "bip" or "bips"). Think of one bp as a penny—just as 100 pennies equals one dollar, 100 bps equals one percentage point. Thus, one bp is .01 percent.

A charge you don't see on your statements or in the firm's fee schedule is a 12(b)1 fee. It's the rule number from the Investment Company Act of 1940 that allows mutual funds to charge a fee for marketing, distribution, and investor services. The fee is deducted from your account daily, which is why you won't see it on your monthly statement. These fees can vary significantly, ranging from 0.25% to 1% annually, depending on the fund. (ETFs generally, unless actively managed, don't charge 12(b)1 fees.) Over time, these costs can add up, reducing the overall return on your investment. Read the company's prospectus, which outlines fees, expenses, and distribution charges.

"Those who know do better than those who don't."

✓ Record your thoughts and ideas from this lesson that you want to incorporate into your investment strategy.

Self-Test Lesson Ten

Control Costs at All Costs!

1. When you invest, you expect your investment to increase in value; however, you must recognize the __________ vs. __________ concept. The greater risk may translate into more __________ *or* more __________.
2. Although market risk can devastate the value of your account, there is another way you can experience a surprising loss in value— __________ fees and other expenses. Therefore, you must control all __________.
3. Never buy a "__________" (commission-based) mutual fund. It's an investment that charges a percentage of the invested amount up front.
4. When you hire a __________ advisor (a no-commission advisor), she will charge a fee as her and her broker/dealers' compensation.
5. A standard annual management fee for invested assets is __________ to __________ % (sometimes negotiable).

6. Do-it-yourself investors save on management fees, but they __________ __________ on the expertise of a __________ professional.
7. There are other fees, and when they're less than 1%, they are called basis __________(s) or bp(s) (pronounced as "bip" or "bips"). Think of one bp as a penny—just as __________ pennies equals one dollar, 100 bps equals one percentage point. Thus, one bp is __________ percent.
8. A charge you don't see on your firm's monthly statements or fee schedule is a "__________ __________."
9. These fees can vary significantly, ranging from __________% to __________% annually, depending on the mutual fund.

LESSON ELEVEN

Scrap Modern Portfolio Theory

TAKE MY ADVICE, scrap Modern Portfolio Theory (MPT). Stay with me for a few minutes; we'll reenter the weeds.

A brilliant American economist named Harry Markowitz devised the Modern Portfolio Theory in 1952. He won the Nobel Memorial Prize in Economic Sciences in 1990. His theory seemed plausible—when some asset categories decline, others rise.

The following is a brief overview of the MPT process. Think of it as a two-step procedure.

Step One: Select asset sectors or categories. MPT mandates investing a percentage in various sectors (e.g., real estate, bonds, commodities, shares in international, emerging markets; U.S. investments in large, mid-size, small, growth, and value companies).

It sounds simple, and it's a format that financial advisors have tried to use for decades. They've adopted a version of MPT as the basis of portfolio construction, replacing the outdated formula of mixing stocks and "fixed income" (cash and bonds), based on the investor's age, (e.g., at age 65, allocate 65 percent in bonds, the balance in stocks to offset inflation, then increase the bond percentage every five years).

Step Two: Calculate the percentage allocated to each sector/category. (See sectors/categories for your sleep-number in Chapter Twelve.) Creating the "Efficient Frontier" is represented on a graph. The vertical line, the Y-axis, represents the "expected return." The horizontal line, the X-axis, represents the "standard deviation" or risk level. Before creating the Efficient Frontier, you need tons of "historical data": returns, volatility, correlations, etc. MPT advises plotting each investment on the graph using the above information to determine the best-suited portfolio for achieving your risk objective.

One of the things I've learned during my 30 years as a Certified Financial Planner™ was this: **When the stock market crashes,** most asset categories tend to fall. Some decline more sharply than others, such as Emerging Markets and Small-Company stocks. Assets that don't usually perform well when the stock market rises—like gold—tend to lag during bull markets. **For example**, from 1990 to 2020, gold increased by approximately 375%, while the S&P 500 gained about 1,460%, including reinvested dividends. (Source: Historical data from Standard & Poor's and analysis by reputable financial firms, such as Morningstar.) Those asset groups could create a drag on the portfolio's performance. Another issue with MPT is that it offers too many asset choices, which can confuse investors.

Here's your homework assignment: Search online for a description of MPT and how to create an "Efficient Frontier", which is based on historical data. However, from my perspective, there's a problem. And it's a BIG one. The historical data is just that: historical. As a young advisor, **I learned I couldn't trust historical data to be repeated consistently.**

As you complete this lesson, I want you to know that when my rewarding career began, mentors advised me that my client accounts should be allocated as stipulated in the MPT. They said it was an up-to-date method for constructing a portfolio. As I mentioned earlier, I followed those instructions to the best of my ability. Over many years, I gained valuable experience and saw flaws in MPT. In Lesson Twelve, I'll explain how I can help you compensate for those flaws.

Your needs may change over time, and so should your investment selections. This is the reason you must recalculate your sleep-number classification each January. Then, using your sleep-number, allocate your portfolio with specific percentages to the appropriate categories suggested in Lesson Twelve. This flexible approach enables you to control your investment strategy, making it easier to understand. **My best advice** would be to focus on simplicity.

✓ Record your thoughts and ideas from this lesson that you want to incorporate into your investment strategy.

Self-Test Lesson Eleven

Scrap Modern Portfolio Theory

1. A brilliant man named Harry Markowitz devised the __________ __________ __________ (MPT) in 1952.
2. Think of MPT as a __________ - __________ process.
3. Step One: Select asset __________ or __________.
4. Step Two: Calculate the __________ allocated to each sector/category.
5. When the stock market crashes, most asset categories tend to __________.
6. Some __________ much worse than others.
7. Another issue with MPT is that there are too many asset __________ that confuse investors.
8. Here's your homework assignment: Search online for a description of MPT and how to create an "Efficient Frontier."

a. What did you learn?

____

____

____

____

9. There is a problem with MPT. And it's a BIG one. The __________ __________ is just historical.
10. You should calculate your __________-__________ classification each year.

✓ Write a brief description of how you see this topic impacting the way you structure your portfolio.

____

____

____

____

____

____

____

____

____

____

____

____

____

____

____

____

____

LESSON TWELVE

Build Your Perfect Portfolio

GOOD NEWS: YOU'VE completed eleven lessons, congratulations, this means you're more knowledgeable about investing your hard-earned money than when you started. So, use what you've learned to finish this course, and modify your investment allocations based on what you've studied.

It's time to organize your thoughts and build what you deem to be **your perfect portfolio** by investing your available dollars in different asset groups. This is what financial advisors refer to as diversification.

If you haven't had time to complete your risk evaluation (sleep-number), drill in Lesson Six, it's time. **Please do it now.** Skillfully role-play the exercise to get a true feel for how you would react when your account balance sinks as you imagine the stock market crashing. You'll be more willing to accept a certain amount of risk after identifying how you feel emotionally about the potential investment losses you might suffer. Then, when you do, you can sit tight, remain patient, and be better prepared to "hang in there" as the stock market continues its uncontrollable lifecycle.

What sleep-number felt the most acceptable? If, for example, you decided you could endure a 10 to 17% portfolio loss, you're an Engaged investor, which means you should put 35% of your dollars in stock and 65% in fixed income.

Sleep-Number Category	Stock/Fixed Income
Careful	25/75
Engaged	35/65
Traditional	55/45
Seasoned	75/25
Determined	95/5

Find your sleep-number category from the above chart and highlight it. Then, divide your investable dollars according to the appropriate allocation chart below.

You may question the validity of the Sleep-Number chart, which implies that all investors have a sleep number that would place them in one of five risk groups. Your observation is on target; however, these five categories are a starting point. Fine-tune your asset distribution into as many asset groups as you like, but maintain your sleep-number percentages within reason.

Adjust the fixed income percentage to allow for the correct amount of bonds and cash. **Under normal circumstances,** you would put no more than 5% in cash. However, in some years (early 2024, for example), fixed-income assets can be volatile. If the federal government's spending is uncontrolled, it might cause inflation, prompting the Federal Reserve to raise rates to control it. Remember that when interest rates increase, bond values typically decrease. **(The opposite of that is also true.)** Therefore, position your fixed income percentage in cash or very short-term bonds until rates remain steady with minimal fluctuations. If you're reading these instructions after rates have stabilized, follow the allocation percentages suggested for each portfolio.

1. Careful – 25% Stock / 75% Fixed Income

Asset Category	Percentage
Large Growth	5
Large Value	20
Mid Growth	0
Mid Value	0
Small Growth	0
Small Value	0
Invest. Grade Bond	70
High-Yield Bond	0
Cash	5
Total	100

These charts suggest examples of the percentages to invest in the different asset classifications. However, you may want to go one step further and search online to see if a "trend" is outperforming the stock market. For example, are emerging market stocks trending higher or lower?

2. Engaged – 35% Stock / 65% Fixed Income

Asset Category	Percentage
Large Growth	10
Large Value	25
Mid Growth	0
Mid Value	0
Small Growth	0
Small Value	0
Invest. Grade Bond	60
High-Yield Bond	0
Cash	5
Total	100

3. Traditional – 55% Stock / 45% Fixed Income

Asset Category	Percentage
Large Growth	20
Large Value	10
Mid Growth	7
Mid Value	8
Small Growth	4
Small Value	6
Invest. Grade Bond	40
High-Yield Bond	0
Cash	5
Total	100

4. Seasoned – 75% Stock / 25% Fixed Income

Asset Category	Percentage
Large Growth	30
Large Value	10
Mid Growth	10
Mid Value	10
Small Growth	8
Small Value	7
Invest. Grade Bond	15
High-Yield Bond	5
Cash	5
Total	100

5. Determined – 95% Stock / 5% Fixed Income

Asset Category	Percentage
Large Growth	30
Large Value	27
Mid Growth	13
Mid Value	10
Small Growth	8
Small Value	7
Invest. Grade Bond	0
High-Yield Bond	0
Cash	5
Total	100

As shown in the above charts, this represents a straightforward allocation of dollars across various asset categories. You may have recognized the absence of international and emerging market investments. I took all of my clients out of those two asset categories in the fall of 2007. I still believe U.S. companies are the best and safest investment option. Keep in mind that non-U.S. stocks tend to be more volatile. However, it's up to you to assess the current environment and determine whether to include them in your portfolio.

After you finish this task, you may have other ideas for adjusting the percentages to match what you believe is your perfect portfolio. **If you're a do-it-yourself investor,** you must perform adequate research before selecting investments. When you have an advisor, you should research the portfolio she has created to ensure it fits your sleep-number and current market circumstances. Be aware that research can be a daunting task. There are plenty of websites available if you're inclined. (Search online for: Investment Research Websites.)

Important information: The regulators refer to your name, address, social security number, and financial records as **Personally Identifiable Information (PII).** Websites with PII must have strong passwords, which should be changed every 90 days. **The problem?** The passwords that are tough to hack are often hard to remember. Security experts say not to write your passwords on a pad of paper next to your computer. To make matters worse, we are told that each website with PII should have a different password. It's a nightmare.

No system works for everyone, but the following may help you solve this everyday problem.

Step 1 – For non-PII websites, create a "master password" using a combination of letters, numbers, and special characters in an order you will never forget. Never. An example would be to use a special character (#, $, *, etc.) and then add a series of letters and number combinations that you will, again, never forget. I've used my best friend's address, when we were kids. (Or use your favorite car-year and model because it has numbers and letters and one upper-case letter, e.g., 1989 Ford). Here's an example using an address, 1451#ElmSt. Utilize the same format as your master password for all websites that don't have PII.

Step 2 – For websites with PII, insert identifier initials or codes to distinguish each account. An easy-to-remember code would be to use the website's first three letters in either lowercase, uppercase, or a combination. An example of a master password for your American Express account could be ame1251#ElmSt. This structure would eliminate confusion about using a different password for each website. Just change the prefix for each site.

Step 3 – Websites containing PII should be changed every 90 days. The solution for that is simple. Add numbers indicating the quarter and the year in any position, for example, ame1251#ElmSt425, for the fourth quarter of 2025. Then, change it for each quarter. Be consistent.

Step 4 - Create a code or reminder that helps you recall how you built your master password. For example, I once used "friend's address" as my cue for **1251#ElmSt**. If my account was at Bank of America, I'd add "ban" to the front—**ban1251#ElmSt**—and then attach the quarter and year so I could update it every 90 days. That would make it **ban1251#ElmSt425**. Easy peasy—and strong.

Keep a list of each website, noting whether its password includes the quarter/year code (QYR). That's it—simple and effective. Most importantly, always use the same format for every account, and think twice before storing your passwords in an online program.

✓ This is another important chapter. So, don't trust your memory. Record your ideas of how you want to structure your investment strategy for future use.

Self-Test Lesson Twelve

Your Perfect Portfolio

1. Have you found your sleep-number? _____ Yes _____ No
2. What level is it? __________
3. It's time to organize your thoughts and build what you deem to be your __________ __________ by investing your available dollars in different __________ groups.
4. Divide your investable dollars according to the appropriate __________ chart.

(Make copies of these pages for future use.)

Asset Category	Percentage
Large Growth	
Large Value	
Mid Growth	
Mid Value	
Small Growth	
Small Value	
Invest. Grade Bond	
High-Yield Bond	
Cash	
Total	

5. You may question the validity of the above, which implies all investors have a sleep-number that would put them in one of only __________ __________ __________.
6. Your observation is on target; however, these __________ __________ are a starting point.
7. Adjust the __________ __________ percentage to allow for an appropriate amount of bonds and cash.
8. Therefore, position your fixed income percentage in __________ or very __________-__________ bonds until rates remain steady with minimal fluctuations.
9. You have learned in "theory" that __________ stocks are less volatile than __________ stocks.
10. You recognized the absence of __________ and __________ market investments.
11. If you're a do-it-yourself investor, you must perform adequate __________ before selecting investments.

12. When you have an advisor, you should research the portfolio she has created to ensure it fits your ________-________ and current market circumstances.
13. The regulators refer to your name, address, social security number, and financial records as ________ ________ ________ (PII).
14. Create a master password for each of your websites.
    a. Step 1. Select an old address ____________________
       ____
       i. I've used my best friend's home address when we were kids.
    b. Step 2. Add identifier code for websites with PII ________
       ____
       i. The first three letters of the URL. (Wells Fargo could be—wel.)
    c. Step 3. Add a quarter and year to make it easy to change in ________ ________. (425 for the last quarter of 2025).
    d. Step 4. Create a code or reminder that helps you recall how you built your master password. ________________
       ____

For example: friend's address.

LESSON THIRTEEN

Employ Basic Tax Strategies

AN IMPORTANT CONSIDERATION when investing money is judging how to employ basic tax strategies. So, in this lesson, I will introduce you to some of the significant differences between taxable and tax-deferred investment accounts to help you understand how to take advantage of something beneficial—**the zero tax bracket** and how it relates to the taxation of long-term capital gains (LTCG) assets in taxable investment accounts.

The information below is based on the **Big Beautiful Bill Act,** as enacted on July 4, 2025. But Congress will likely make changes down the road. When they do, come back to what you've learned here and adjust your strategy as needed.

Your primary income is what the IRS refers to as "ordinary income." I call it **"regular income"** for example: wages, bank interest, dividends,

Social Security, pension income, and so on. Current tax rates on regular income range from 10% to 37% for both single filers and married couples filing jointly.

Tax Table for Single Filers

$0 – $11,925	10%
$11,926 – 48,475	12%
$48,476 – $103,350	22%
$103,351 – $197,300	24%
$197,301 – $250,525	32%
$250,526 – $626,350	35%
Over $626,351	37%

Tax Table for Married Couples Filing Jointly

$0 – $23,850	10%
$23,851 – $96,950	12%
$96,951 – $206,700	22%
$206,701 – $394,600	24%
$394,601 – $501,050	32%
$501,051 – $751,600	35%
$751,601 and over	37%

There is an additional **0.9% Medicare tax** on income and a 3.8% tax on **Net Investment Income Tax (NIIT)** for high-income earners. These two taxes were introduced by the **Affordable Care Act** to help fund Medicare and health care reform. (If you have income over $200,000 as a single filer or $250,000 as a married couple filing jointly, make sure to search online for details on these two taxes.) Readers with very high incomes may be unable to use some of the following tax-saving maneuvers. However, you should give it a try.

Note: Your tax bracket and your effective (or average) tax rate are not the same—except possibly if you're in the lowest tax bracket. Your tax bracket refers to the highest rate applied to a portion of your income, while your effective tax rate is the overall percentage of your taxable income that you pay in taxes. As you move into higher tax brackets, only the income within each bracket is taxed at that bracket's rate. To calculate your effective tax rate, divide the total tax you owe by your taxable income.

Formula:

Effective Tax Rate = (Total Tax ÷ Taxable Income) × 100

You should adopt a different investment approach for "taxable" (non-qualified) accounts versus "tax-deferred" (qualified) accounts, such as 401(k)s, IRAs, and 403(b)s. You will also pay regular tax on these accounts, but that payment is deferred until you withdraw your funds. The following will help you understand the process.

Taxable investment accounts are those that you pay tax on each year when there is a taxable event. Such an event will occur when selling stock, whether at a loss or a gain, and in most instances, they are reported in the year of the sale.* You might also receive a distribution of capital gains and interest/dividends, which are taxable.

Taxable investment accounts don't enjoy tax deferral, but they do have different "favorable" tax rules. You must understand the main differences to decide when a taxable investment account might make sense as an alternative to a tax-deferred investment or when to use a combined action plan.

Most of your income is taxed using regular income tax rates. However, when you sell a capital asset, like stock, in a taxable account, the tax is based on the lower capital gains tax rate.

A massive tax benefit exists in a taxable account: capital-gains assets are taxed at 0, 15, or 20%, depending on your taxable income level.

Important Note: This favorable tax rate is available on assets held more than one year including qualified dividends. Remember to calculate the 0.9% and 3.8% additional tax for high-income taxpayers.

What is capital gains tax? It's a tax you pay on the profit you receive when you sell certain assets, like stock and real property. (Primary residence exclusion: If you sell your home and meet ownership and use tests, you may exclude up to $250,000 for single filers or $500,000 for married couples filing jointly of the gain from tax.) Collectibles, such as art, stamps, and coins, are taxed at a higher rate.

Long-Term Capital Gains Rates for a Single Filer

$0 – $48,350	0%
$48,351 – $533,400	15%
$533,401 and over	20%

As you can see, the zero percent bracket is a huge benefit for savvy investors. A single filer pays no long-term capital gains tax when their taxable income is $48,350 or less—and up to $96,700 for those married filing jointly (MFJ).

Long-Term Capital Gains Rates for Married Filing Jointly

$0 – $96,700	0%
$96,701 – $597,850	15%
$597,851 and over	20%

Think of the possibilities. This part of the tax code will, under the right circumstances, allow you to reap significant profits. Let's take a look at some possibilities.

Tax-savings strategy example:

Step One: Invest $50,000 in a growth ETF that increases in value to $60,000.

Step Two: Calculate all your regular income plus long-term gains minus deductions. If you don't exceed $48,350 for a single filer or $96.700 for married couples filing jointly (including the profit after selling the ETF), your tax bill on the gain will be zero. Yes, zero.

Step Three: It gets better. You can reinvest the sale's proceeds in the same or another investment, and guess what? You just increased your adjusted tax basis in your investment to $60,000 without paying a tax. Continue this three-step process as your account continues to grow and your taxable income does not exceed the maximum income levels mention above. Over time, your adjusted tax basis will become a significantly larger number. Then, when you need the money, you can withdraw those prior tax-free gains as adjusted tax basis without being subject to a tax.

Someone might say you can't reinvest in the same or a similar investment for thirty days. They are referring to the "Wash Sale Rule." However, the Wash Sale Rule only applies to sales resulting in a loss, not a gain.

If your taxable income exceeds the $48,350 or $96,700 limits but is close, consider looking for losses in your taxable investment accounts. Then, you can **"harvest"** (sell) them to lower your taxable income. You can deduct losses equal to gains and use up to $3,000 in excess losses each year to offset regular income. This technique may get you to the zero capital gains tax bracket.

The tricky or secret part, or whatever you want to call it, is "controlling" your income to keep it below the $48,350 and $96,700 zero tax brackets mentioned above. Controlling your income is a crucial strategy for winning your battle with the IRS.

This strategy also yields benefits for higher-income earners with incomes above the zero-percent thresholds, as the 15% and 20% tax rates on capital gains are significantly lower than the regular (ordinary) income tax rates.

Suppose it's November, and as a single filer, you've calculated your taxable income at $50,000. You're thinking of selling an ETF with a $10,000 gain—but you want to stay within the zero percent long-term capital gains bracket. You're $11,650 over the limit. The good news? You've kept accurate records of income and deductions all year, so now your goal is to find $11,650 in additional deductions. But how?

Here are possible strategies if you itemize deductions—one is called "accelerating" deductions. For example:

1. Pay your state's estimated tax payment in December instead of January.

2. Make next year's charitable donations before December 31.
3. Accelerate elective medical expenses—like surgeries, eyeglasses, or hearing aids—but only if they exceed 7.5% of your adjusted gross income (AGI). Only the amount above that threshold is deductible.

An alternative option would be to decide whether it would make sense to bunch deductions into next year, which is the opposite of accelerating deductions.

Whether you itemized or use the standard deduction consider the following:

1. Increasing contributions to tax-deferred accounts like an IRA, 401(k) or 403(b).
2. Health Savings Account (HSA) Contributions
3. If you have a high-deductible health plan (HDHP), contributions to an HSA are **"above-the-line" deductions**, meaning they reduce AGI.
4. **Self-Employed SEP IRA or Solo 401(k)**
5. If you're self-employed or have side income, these plans let you deduct large retirement contributions **without itemizing**.
    a. Self-Employed Health Insurance Deduction
        i. If you're self-employed and pay your own health insurance premiums, you may deduct them directly from your AGI—even if you use the standard deduction. Deduction cannot exceed your net profit from self-employment (see Schedule C rules).

6. **Student Loan Interest Deduction**
   a. Up to **$2,500** of interest paid on qualified student loans can be deducted from AGI, depending on income phaseouts.
7. **Educator Expenses**
   a. Teachers and qualified educators can deduct up to **$300** (or $600 if married and both are teachers) for classroom supplies. (Reduces AGI.)
8. **Losses from Sole Proprietorships or Rentals**
   a. Net operating losses (Schedule C or E) flow through and can lower AGI.

Strategy Alert: Tax-Free Bond Strategy

- **High Earners Choose Municipal Bonds**: High earners invest in tax-free municipal bonds to avoid federal (and often state) taxes on interest. A 5% Muni bond beats a 7% taxable corporate bond after taxes (e.g., 4.41% after 37% tax).
- **Lower Earners Prefer Corporate Bonds**: Lower earners opt for corporate bonds for higher yields, as their low tax rate means less tax impact (e.g., 7% corporate bond yields 6.16% after 12% tax).
- **Munis for Lower Earners' Tax-Free Gains**: To maximize the 0% capital gains rate (taxable income up to $48,350 single or $96,700 joint), lower earners can use municipal bonds. Tax-exempt Muni bond interest keeps taxable income low, ensuring investment profits (ETF sales) stay tax-free.
  - o For example, if a single filer has $25,000 in wages and $10,000 in Muni bond interest, their taxable income (after a $15,750 standard deduction) is $9,250. Selling an ETF

for a $10,000 profit keeps their taxable income at $19,250 well below the $48,350 threshold, so the profit is tax-free.

- **Why It Works**: Munis save high earners on taxes and help lower earners keep taxable income low for tax-free capital gains. Corporate bonds suit lower earners for higher yields when taxes are less of a concern.

Tip: Consult a tax professional/financial advisor to tailor these strategies to your federal and state tax rules.

Tax tactics can be game-changers, and **a combination may help you achieve zero tax on your capital gains.**

When making investment decisions in taxable accounts, be careful not to allow the tax tail to wag the investment strategy dog. In other words, investment policy decisions generally come first and tax decisions second. However, this rule doesn't mean you should never prioritize tax tactics over investment decisions.

Tax-deferred investment accounts offer significant tax advantages, which is why most financial advisors, money managers, and many investors prefer to invest in taxable accounts only after their available tax-deferred accounts (e.g., IRAs, 401(k)s, 403(b)s) are fully maxed out. Here are three main advantages:

1. immediate tax deduction
2. tax-deferred growth, and
3. the ability to make trades without current taxation.

The disadvantage, though, is when you withdraw tax-deferred money, it's generally** taxed as regular (ordinary) income, which is at a higher rate. Also, be forewarned—tax-deferred accounts have strict IRS rules you must not violate. **Be careful.**

As mentioned, investing in a tax-deferred account allows you to secure a tax deduction based on your contribution. The result is tax savings equal to your tax rate. If, for example, you pay a 12% tax rate, you'll save $840 in taxes on a $7,000 IRA contribution. **Higher tax brackets result in greater tax savings.** The long-term deferral of those tax dollars is a big plus. Tax deferral means that the taxes you would have sent to the IRS remain in your account and, over time, may grow as the market experiences its bumpy upward climb. You can also execute buy and sell trades in a tax-deferred account without immediate tax consequences. For example, when you sell all or part of an S&P 500 ETF position in an IRA account, **you can't report a loss,** nor are you required to report a gain.

You might wonder why you can't deduct losses from your qualified accounts. It's because you've never paid taxes on those dollars, and you won't until you withdraw them.

Remember, contributions to tax-deferred investment accounts get you a tax deduction, saving tax based on your tax rate. All buy and sell trades are insulated from taxation. Furthermore, when those assets grow, they are growing in a tax-sheltered environment until you take withdrawals. However, withdrawals are taxed as regular income, not at capital-gains rates. As a result, you pay a higher tax rate. Unfortunately, you don't know what the rate will be when you withdraw money. Future rates may be higher.

* * *

While you're LEARNING about how to control income, it isn't far-fetched, at this point, to suggest you think about a different higher-level strategy to achieve an additional goal: **Contribute to a Roth IRA**.

Current tax law allows you to convert tax-deferred retirement accounts to a Roth IRA at any age. There are strict rules you must follow, but there are significant advantages to converting. Distributions are tax-free, and you don't have Required Minimum Distributions (RMDs) each year when you reach age 73. It's a big deal **(study the next paragraph).** However, you must pay the tax based on your tax bracket when executing the conversion. It's a tough pill to swallow, **but maybe it's good medicine in the long term.** Investors *with* tax-deferred retirement accounts must start withdrawing their required minimum distributions (RMDs) and pay the regular tax when they reach age 73. This forced distribution could be problematic and prevent your strategy of selling capital gains assets in the zero bracket.

Furthermore, the increased income may cause your social security benefits to be taxed at a higher rate. The additional income can also trigger an increase in your Medicare premiums. Search online for 'Medicare Parts A & B premiums and deductibles'. You'll see that as your taxable income increases, so do your premiums.

Here's why a Roth IRA conversion can sometimes be a smart move:

> With the right plan, you can convert part of a traditional IRA to a Roth IRA while staying in a lower tax bracket—and avoid paying higher tax rates than necessary.

I call this the **Bracket Bounce Bailout Conversion Process (BBBCP)**. The idea is simple:

1. Know your current tax bracket.
2. Convert just enough from your IRA to a Roth IRA so you "bounce up" to the top of your current bracket—but stop before you cross into the next, higher rate.

Example:

- A **single filer** with $40,000 in taxable income could convert **up to $8,475** and still remain in the 12% bracket.
- A **married couple filing jointly** with $70,000 in taxable income could convert **up to $26,950** before moving into the 22% bracket.

Doing this in stages over multiple years can keep your tax bill lower while shifting more of your retirement savings into a Roth, where qualified withdrawals are tax-free.

Because tax laws change, it's wise to work with a qualified professional who can help you adjust your strategy when needed.

Keep good records. A comprehensive paper trail is the most effective defense against an IRS audit.

* You may deduct up to $3,000 in losses against regular income after netting gains and losses. Any balance must be a carryover to the following year(s).

** Net unrealized appreciation or NUA, which applies to special tax treatment for company stock held in a retirement plan like a 401(k). It can be taxed as capital gains when you follow strict IRS rules. This is a complicated section of the tax code and should only be undertaken with the help of a qualified professional.

✓ Record your thoughts and ideas from this lesson that you want to incorporate into your investment strategy.

Self-Test Lesson Thirteen

Employ Basic Tax Strategies

1. An important consideration when investing money is judging how to ________ ________ tax strategies.
2. Your primary income is what the IRS refers to as "________ ________."
3. I call it "________ ________," for example: wages, bank interest, dividends, Social Security, pension income, etc.
4. Current tax rates for regular income range from ________ to ________ percent for single filers and married couples filing jointly.
5. There is an additional ________ percent Medicare tax and ________ percent tax for Net Investment Income for high-income earners.
6. Your "________ ________" and "average or effective tax rate" are two different numbers unless you're in the lowest tax bracket.

7. To calculate your "effective tax rate," divide your __________ __________ into your actual tax then x 100.
8. You should adopt a different investment approach for "__________" (non-qualified) accounts versus "__________-__________" (qualified) accounts.
9. Taxable investment accounts don't enjoy tax __________ but have a different set of "__________" tax rules.
10. A massive tax benefit exists in a taxable account: "__________ __________" assets are taxed at 0, 15, or 20%, depending on your taxable income level.
11. Important Note: This favorable tax rate is available on assets held for over __________ year including qualified dividends
12. A single filer's capital gains tax rate is 0% when their taxable income does not exceed $__________ for a Single Filer or $__________ for Married Couples Filing Jointly.
13. Tax savings strategy example:
    a. **Step One**: Invest $ __________ in a growth ETF that increases in value to $ __________.
    b. **Step Two**: Calculate all your regular income plus long-term gains minus deductions. If you don't exceed $__________ for a single filer or $__________ for married couples filing jointly (including the profit after selling the ETF), your tax bill on the gain will be zero. Yes, zero.
    c. **Step Three:** It gets better. You can __________ the sale's proceeds in the same or another investment, and guess what? You just increased the adjusted __________ __________ on your investment without paying a tax.
14. If your taxable income exceeds the $48,475 or $96,950 limits, but you're close, look for __________ in your taxable invest-

ment accounts. Then, you can "__________" (sell) them to lower your taxable income. You can deduct losses equal to gains and use up to $__________ in excess losses to offset regular income.

15. "__________" your income is a significant opportunity you can use to win your battle with the IRS.
16. Suppose it's November, and as a single filer, you've calculated your taxable income at $__________. You're thinking of selling an ETF with a $__________ gain—but you want to stay within the zero percent long-term capital gains bracket.
17. You're $11,650 over the limit. The good news? You've kept accurate records of __________ and __________ all year, so now your goal is to find $__________ in additional deductions. But how?
18. List three possible tax strategies for taxpayers who itemize deductions:
    a. __________
    b. __________
    c. __________
19. An alternative option would be to decide whether it would make sense to __________ deductions into next year, which is the opposite of __________ deductions.
20. List the eight possible tax strategies for taxpayers who use the Standard Deduction:
    1. __________
    2. __________
    3. __________
    4. __________
    5. __________

6. ______
7. ______
8. ______

21. High earners invest in tax-free ______ bonds to avoid federal (and often state) ______ on interest.
22. To maximize the 0% capital gains rate (taxable income up to $48,350 single or $96,700 joint), ______ ______ can use municipal bonds.
23. Munis save high earners on taxes and help ______ ______ keep taxable income low for tax-free capital gains.
24. Corporate bonds suit ______ ______ for higher yields when taxes are less of a concern.
25. Current tax law allows you to convert tax-deferred retirement accounts to a ______ ______ at any age.
26. Roth distributions are tax-free, and you don't have ______ ______ ______ (RMDs) each year.
27. You must pay tax based on your ______ ______ when executing the conversion.
28. Investors with tax-deferred retirement accounts must start withdrawing their ______ ______ ______ and pay the regular tax when they reach age ______.
29. Increased income may also cause your ______ ______ benefits to be taxed at a higher rate.
30. The additional income can also trigger your ______ premiums to increase. These are some reasons ______ ______ conversions may make sense.
31. Is there a possible solution? Yes. I call it the ______ ______ ______ Conversion Process (BBBCP).

32. For example, a single taxpayer with $40,000 of taxable income could ________ up by converting $__________ of an IRA to a Roth IRA before going into the 22% bracket.
33. Married couples filing jointly with $70,000 of taxable income could bounce up by converting $__________ before reaching the 22% bracket.

LESSON FOURTEEN

Hang-in-There?

WALL STREET PROMOTES, in more than a subtle way—call it a warning—that you should achieve an annual portfolio return equal to the S&P 500's. Some say, "If you miss the ten best days of the year, your return is cut in half." This is the message to substantiate the "hang-in-there" directive when the stock market is crashing.

Many studies have found the opposite to be true. If you miss the ten *worst* days of the year, your returns will be higher. **Here's the truth:** It's impossible to foretell the future, and no one can position their portfolio to capture the ten best days and avoid the ten worst days. So, what should you do? Keep reading.

Earlier, I mentioned that I would focus your attention on something the industry doesn't discuss, my secret in the sauce, which may be your most important investment consideration. **What is it?** "Your emotions."

Do you agree? Of course, your emotions play a critical role in your portfolio's results.

Wall Street generally ignores this vital factor. They think investors can control their emotions. Many can't. Their strategy is presented as though you're in a contest with the S&P 500 or another benchmark. They conclude you're losing money if you don't match its return. **They're wrong.** You're only losing hypothetical money. Not your money. The goal of matching the S&P 500's return is unrealistic. Think about this: You'd have to be at sleep-number **Determined**, the most aggressive, and have 100 percent of your portfolio *in* the S&P 500 to mirror its return. And you don't want to match its return when the S&P 500 is going in the wrong direction.

Wall Street ignores a significant investor concern, their "Worry-Meter." It's the elephant in the room. Regular investors like you and me have said: **"We're three times more afraid of losing money than increasing our account balance."** Interesting. Scrutinize the above statement for a minute. It reeks of emotional stress and anxiety.

As a younger person with a long time horizon, staying invested when stocks crash makes sense. However, it's not a good idea if you're a worrier, an older investor, in the 75+-year-old group, or if the market is crashing as a result of a systemic risk.

"The stock market will come back." Yes, it will. But when? More importantly, what "EMOTIONS" do you have to endure in the meantime? How much sleep will you lose while you wait? **Sleepless nights can cause health concerns,** and one is called ***moneylossitis.*** It's a disease affecting the nervous system that causes many symptoms, including impaired mental ability, persistent headaches, weakness or loss of muscle strength, stomach tightness, and other disorders.

Earlier, you learned that financial advisors are taught to encourage clients to allocate their investments according to their risk tolerance. **The problem,** you may remember, is that hypothetical risk questions are theoretical. They don't hit the bull's eye to reveal how you feel emotionally, and to weaken the process further, the questions are usually administered when you're in a non-emotional, stress-free state of mind.

The importance of the exercise you completed in **Lesson Six** can't be overstated. It's where you calculated your sleep-number.

Assuming you could role-play the experience as though the stock market was getting hammered **you'd have a reasonably accurate result.** At what level did you feel calm? Sleep-numbers 4 and 5 are the most aggressive and are for investors who can weather down markets better than most. Sleep-numbers 1 and 2 are more conservative, and sleep-number 3 is the middle of the road, similar to the stock allocation recommended by many financial advisors.

Now you've completed the "sleep-number" questions. **You have the antidote to *moneylossitis*** and a better chance of dialing down your emotional reaction when the stock market goes negative. When you **precisely** role-play the risk tolerance exercise, the "hang in there" until the market rebounds may be your best option. **I say that with the assumption that you have found your sleep-number** and your asset allocation is one you find acceptable.

If you only learn one breakthrough idea from this course, let it be this: Disassociate yourself from the faulty premise that your portfolio should compete with the S&P 500 or any benchmark. In my opinion, the industry warning to "hang in there" shouldn't be followed when there is a systemic risk causing the stock market's downward trajectory, resulting in your "worry meter" hitting the red zone.

Systemic risk is the kind of danger you want to watch for. Often, the stock market reacts negatively to speculation about what *might* happen rather than what *is* happening. Be careful here. Ask yourself: Is there a legitimate, widespread reason for the market to pull back? Is the event likely to cause consumers, businesses, and financial institutions across the economy to pull back activity? If you can answer "yes," that's systemic risk—it affects the entire market, not just individual companies.

Think back to 2008. Do you remember all the bad financial news in mid-September and October? You read about Lehman Brothers and American International Group (AIG) earlier. Others were in the headlines: Bank of America took over Merrill Lynch, Washington Mutual went bankrupt, and Wells Fargo acquired Wachovia. More bad news was in the headlines, but you get my point. **The financial disaster was the result of systemic risk.** The shadowy Wall Streeters recklessly manipulated the subprime lending markets, misrepresenting those securities as AAA (Investment Grade) quality. It was widespread and almost crippled our financial system.

Another critical point that Wall Street never discusses is whether the stock market and your investments rebound together. Or will some asset classes in your portfolio struggle to keep pace? It's worth thinking about.

Your peace of mind is essential. Peace of mind comes at a price. What are you willing to pay? The tradeoff for protecting your money may be a loss of potential return. This point bears repeating: Once you've answered the "sleep number" questions, you'll be better prepared to ride the roller coaster—even when emotional stress and gut-wrenching swings hit hard.

✓ Record your thoughts and ideas from this lesson that you want to incorporate into your investment strategy.

Self-Test Lesson Fourteen

Hang-In-There?

1. Wall Street promotes, in more than a subtle way—call it a warning—that you should achieve an annual portfolio return __________ to the S&P 500's.
2. Some say, "If you miss the __________ best days of the year, your return is cut in half."
3. Many studies have found the opposite to be true. If you missed the ten __________ days of the year, your returns would be higher.
4. Here's the truth: it's __________ to foretell the future, and no one can position their portfolio to capture the ten __________ days and avoid the ten __________ days
5. Earlier, I mentioned that I would focus your attention on something the industry doesn't discuss, my secret in the sauce, which may be your most important investment consideration. What is it? "__________ __________." Do you agree? Of course, your emotions play a critical role in your portfolio's results.

6. Wall Street ignores a significant investor concern, their "__________ __________."
7. Regular investors like you and me have said we're __________ times more afraid of losing money than increasing our account balance.
8. "The Market will come back." Yes, it will. But when? And what "__________" do you have to experience in the meantime?
9. If you only learn one breakthrough idea from this course, let it be this: __________ yourself from the faulty premise that your portfolio should __________ with the S&P 500 or any benchmark.
10. **Systemic risk** is the kind of __________ you want to watch for.
11. Often, the stock market reacts negatively to speculation about what __________ happen rather than what __________ happening.
12. Be careful here. Ask yourself: Is there a __________, widespread reason for the market to pull back?
13. Is the event likely to cause consumers, businesses, and financial institutions across the economy to __________ __________ activity?
14. If you can answer "yes," that's __________ __________—it affects the entire market, not just individual companies.

LESSON FIFTEEN

Have a Well-Thought-Out Plan

IT'S NOT TIMING the stock market, but time in the stock market that results in the growth of your investments. As you have learned, **emotions can often take over,** so it is essential to have a well-thought-out strategy.

Your plan should blend both your intellectual analysis and your emotional instincts. You already know the old rule about not putting all your eggs in one basket. Another equally important rule is: never invest money you can't afford to lose. That means avoiding investments when:

1. Losing the money would harm your financial stability.
2. It would cause significant emotional stress.
3. You don't fully understand how it works—like cryptocurrencies.

You must calculate your sleep-number correctly. Have you? Okay, you've nailed down your sleep-number, so now what? What's your plan? **How should you proceed?** Good questions. It's not Modern Portfolio Theory that Wall Street puts before you. They have your best interests at heart, but their premise disregards your personal feelings, emotions, and ability to sleep at night, which impacts your quality of life.

Be alert, and don't be greedy. Greed is fertilizer and grows fear and financial damage, which you see reflected in your statements. Or do you put those unopened envelopes in the desk drawer when the stock market goes south?

If you have a long-term time horizon (10 years plus), you're better positioned to isolate yourself from the emotional ups and downs and not let negative market moves affect your life. Allow your gut to guide you; go with the flow and ride out down markets when your emotions can handle it. **On the other hand,** if you have a short-term time horizon (one to six years) or "worry" too much about your account value going down, you must make the needed adjustments. Recalculate your sleep-number and, if necessary, reposition your account(s) to a more conservative distribution of stocks, bonds, and cash. It can be a roller coaster ride.

I recall the last time I rode a real roller coaster. The car started chugging up to the top, and as I glanced over, I saw what was coming. It looked like the car was going straight down to the bottom and crash. When it reached the top, it seemed as though it was going to stop, and then suddenly, **hang on,** the car was accelerating downhill at the speed of light, or so it seemed. I still recall the only thought racing through my mind: What am I doing? Have you ever had that feeling? You know what I'm talking about, whether caused by the stock market or an amusement park ride. It's a gut crunch you'll never forget.

Riding the roller coaster is suitable for investors with substantial incomes, healthy reserves, long time horizons, or those who can disassociate themselves from the emotional ups and downs of the financial markets. They can wait it out without pressure and fear. But experience has taught me that they are the exception, not the rule.

Go back to 2008 again. When I met with my clients to discuss my recommended course of action, I said, "I don't know the cause, but a 128-year-old company is bankrupt, and the Federal Reserve is taking control of the largest insurance company in the world. Something terrible is in the wind.

Investors had two choices: (1) "hang in there," ride the roller coaster, or **(2)** reduce their stock holdings." As I've said, they took my recommendation to get out of all stocks and into U.S. Treasury Bonds, rather than reducing the stock percentage. However, **you shouldn't get out of stock willy-nilly**. You must have a valid reason: "a systemic risk" causing negative market volatility. Be careful here. Determining the level of market fluctuations is complex, and nailing down a good reason for the correction may elude you. Then, it could reverse direction without any apparent reason.

Two things would trigger the stock market to lose value: **(1)** "speculation" about bad news and **(2)** actual bad news. In both situations, I'd try to determine the facts: Was speculation or actual negative news (systemic risk) causing companies not to be able to sell their products and services? Then, I would use factual information to make recommendations to my clients.

Good news: The systemic risk problems causing stocks to take a nosedive are few and infrequent, so you can concentrate on living life.

It would be best if you had a well-thought-out strategy. You might aim for an annual growth rate to increase your account's value to the level needed to achieve your desired outcome. Call it *your* benchmark return. You could also factor expected inflation into your plan. Consider your effective income tax rate on taxable accounts, as the IRS expects to receive its share of money each year. Your annual **growth rate target must be realistic.** Aiming for a ten percent return doesn't make sense when you're a Level 1 investor. Your formula must also consider the amount of new money you invest each year.

Alternatively, you may dispense with the complexities of the above and **keep it simple by targeting** a reasonable annual growth rate of 4–8%. Your target rate must align with your sleep-number.

You should measure progress every January to determine whether the return rate for the last twelve months is higher or lower than your target rate. However, you may review or fine-tune your portfolio on a quarterly or semi-annual basis. **I favor quarterly.** But at the very least, an annual review is imperative. Remember the saying, "Those who know do better than those who don't."

When your return rate exceeds your target, you'll have a big smile, but when it's lower, don't agonize. Search your portfolio for evidence telling you which were poor performers or where the losses occurred. Were they consistent with the performance of their peer sector group? Use that information as a gauge to evaluate each investment. **Sell and replace** any position not matching the performance of its peer group. Be sure to assess tax consequences in taxable accounts.

Following trends can be a valuable tool, but overweighing an asset category must not "whack" your allocation out of its original sleep-number structure. **Review Lesson Seven,** where you learned about the differences between Growth and Value stocks, and Lesson Twelve, where you learned how to structure your perfect portfolio. When you follow a trend, you overweight and underweight specific asset categories—keep it within reason. As the saying goes, "Don't go hog wild."

If you're following a trend, you must review progress every three months.

✓ Record your thoughts and ideas from this lesson that you want to incorporate into your investment strategy.

Self-Test Lesson Fifteen

Have a Well-Thought-Out Plan

1. Your plan should involve a coordinated combination of your acquired __________ and __________ thoughts.
2. Another critical rule is don't invest money you can't __________ to lose.
3. Greed is fertilizer, and it grows __________ and __________ damage, which you see reflected in your statements.
4. If you have a long-term time horizon (__________ __________ __________), you're better positioned to isolate yourself from the emotional ups and downs and not let negative market moves affect your life.
5. If you have a __________ - __________ time horizon (one to six years) or "worry" too much about your account value going down, don't be rigid. You must make the necessary adjustments.
6. You shouldn't get out of stock __________ - __________. You must have a valid reason: "a __________ __________" causing negative market volatility.

7. Two things would trigger the S&P 500 to lose value: (1) "__________" about bad news and (2) __________ bad news. In both situations, I'd try to determine the facts.
8. It would be best if you had a well-thought-out strategy. You might __________ an annual growth rate that will advance your account's value to equal what you need to __________ your desired outcome. Call it *your* __________ return.
9. Your annual growth rate target must be realistic. Aiming for a __________ percent return doesn't make sense when you're a __________ __________ investor.
10. You should measure progress __________ to determine whether the last twelve months' return rate is higher or lower than your __________ rate.
11. Following trends can be a valuable tool, but overweighting an asset category must not "__________" your allocation out of its original sleep-number structure.

Final Thoughts

START OVER?

YOU HAVE COMPLETED all 15 lessons. **Congratulations!** What are your final thoughts? Here's a better question: **What are you going to do now?** You have a choice. Read another book? Or will you continue with this course and return to Lesson One to review everything you underlined, highlighted and the self-tests?

Did you keep a notebook with ideas and concepts you wanted to remember and implement? Did you complete all the self-tests? You can make the most of this course if you answer yes to those questions. And you'll make financial progress as a do-it-yourself investor or be better equipped to work with and understand what your financial advisor is doing with your money.

What you have learned is of little importance; it is what you do with what you have learned that measures your worth.

—John F. Cicotte

Guess What?

I Need Your Help!

Someone you know—and countless others you don't—could benefit from the lessons in this course.

Here's how you can help them *and* me:

1. **Leave a Review on Amazon**
   - Go to Amazon.com, search for *Become The Intelligent Investor*, and post your review.
   - In your review, consider sharing:
     (a) How this course improved your ability to manage your investments.
     (b) Whether the teaching was clear, easy to understand, and practical.
     (c) If the lessons were simple to follow and presented in a logical order.

2. **Spread the Word**
    - Share your new investing knowledge with family, friends, and your social media networks.
    - Tell them what insights opened your eyes and boosted your confidence as an investor.

Your support means a great deal. Thank you for helping me inspire more people to take control of their financial future!

Continue Your Journey

Retirement Solved

Discover the Mysteries!
Power, Control, and Happy Times
Beyond Retirement Day

In *Become the Intelligent Investor*, we've focused on clear, practical steps you can take to strengthen your financial life. If you'd like a different kind of learning experience, my companion book, *Retirement Solved: Discover the Mysteries*, blends story and strategy to make retirement planning both engaging and practical.

To give you a sense of how it works, read the following.

IMPORTANT INTRODUCTION

This is a story about people like you with the same hopes, dreams, and fears about the future. It'll help you paint a picture of what you want your retirement to include.

Most chapters consist of two parts: The Story and The Nitty-Gritty. The Story sections expose critical planning problems that you need to be aware of and, when necessary, fix. The Nitty-Gritty sections will simplify and help you understand the objectives and complexities presented in The Story sections.

Throughout The Story section of most chapters, you'll come to know your new friends, Lisa and Mark Dolan. They're confused and worried about retirement coming in nine years. Amazingly, a mystical financial advisor, Ace Sorts, visits Mark in his dreams to teach and inspire him with planning instructions. You'll witness each rich, intense, and simplified tutorial. As you read, ask yourself, could Ace Sorts be a natural person with the power to connect with Mark through his dreams?

(While Lisa and Mark Dolan, Ace Sorts, Chico Jetton, and others feel real as you read their story, they are entirely fictional. Any resemblance to actual people, living or deceased, is purely coincidental. Their experiences are crafted to illustrate important retirement planning lessons, and the story is meant to entertain, inspire, and guide you—not reflect real events.)

You'll also get to know Chico Jetton, CFP®, founder and owner of Chico Jetton Retirement, Inc. Your first introduction to Chico will be in a Nitty-Gritty section—he's helped a do-it-yourself investor who realized he didn't know everything he needed to know.

Chapter 19 reveals Chico's seven-step L.I.F.E. Formula—*Live. Imagine. Focus. Enjoy.*®—a practical and inspiring roadmap designed to help you navigate retirement with purpose and fulfillment.

You picked up this book because you want to learn how to have a better future, which will happen as you absorb the ideas and principles discussed in The Nitty-Gritty sections. This dual approach offers an engaging reading experience, stimulating the receptive regions of your brain with techniques that will invigorate your intellectual juices. You'll experience considerable rewards when you use these easy-to-understand planning tools.

Plotting your future takes preparation, though. Perhaps you are retired or close to retirement, wondering, "What will the rest of my life look like?" Or maybe you're a take-charge younger person who knows it's never too early to map your future. "How do I overcome common obstacles and capture my dream?" you ask. My answer? Conquer everyone's first planning problem—complexity. It's the enemy of execution. Complexity fuels procrastination and confuses your good intentions. Choosing the path of least resistance and doing nothing leads to failure. Don't let the thorny uncertainties ahead stop you from reaching for your rose. Visualize happiness and manage your money to help support your vision.

One dictionary definition of "retire" is to withdraw from active life, from circulation, to go away to a place of privacy, shelter, or seclusion." Retirement is none of those things. Think of retire-ment as a time of "rebirth-ment." A new beginning. A new adventure. It is an exciting journey into the best life can offer. It's a time to reward yourself after years of hard work and self-sacrifice. It's life's dessert. Although different people enjoy different flavors, everyone's recipe has common ingredients. These pages will help channel your thoughts and actions to discover your recipe. They'll help reveal what makes you feel joyful and fulfilled. Instead of letting it slip through your fingers, you will explore whatever feels left undone and how to capture it. It's a way to chart your life after paychecks stop.

This book is neither a panacea nor a guarantee of an implied outcome. Nothing in these pages should be construed as promissory. Instead, you can use this story to help inspire you to study the unknown to learn how to navigate this exciting chapter of your life, whether it's around the corner or years in the future. It'll encourage you with powerful ideas, concepts, and motivation. You'll learn how to nourish your aspirations to grow them into a relaxed and pleasurable lifestyle. Your results will depend on your choices and the specific action steps you complete. Your future happiness depends on you, no one else, and your implementation of the action steps you're about to learn.

You don't want a book full of unfamiliar financial and investment vocabulary, so, as much as possible, you will see the use of technical terms and financial jargon minimized and a bold attempt to simplify confusing material. However, be on notice that the true scope of retirement planning is complicated.

My purpose in writing this book is "to give you basic tools to help you pursue your financial and retirement goals." You can achieve your retirement dream. Immerse yourself in the wisdom these pages teach. Internalize the lessons. Strive to fulfill your ambitions. Believe that the ability to make it happen comes with knowledge, positive expectations, and follow-through!

All this information will enable you to prepare to experience your most thrilling journey: life after work.